LOVE
the Word that heals

LOVE
the Word that heals

Amulree Paperback No. 4

published by
ARTHUR JAMES LIMITED
The Drift, Evesham,
Worcs., England

First Edition 1981

© Denis Duncan 1981

*All rights reserved by the publishers
Arthur James Limited, of Evesham, Worcs., England*

Duncan, Denis
Love, the word that heals. — (Amulree
paperback; no. 4)
1. Christian life 2. Love
I. Title
248'.4   BV4639
ISBN 0-85305-231-X

Printed by **Gibbons Barford** Wolverhampton

PREFACE

The Word that heals is LOVE

In my recent book, *Creative Silence* (Amulree Paperback No. 1, Arthur James), I said that I hoped, at some time, to deal with all the qualities listed there under the heading "The Harvest of the Spirit" by devoting a volume to each one. The hope remains, though the task can only be a long-term one! I make a start with the first and greatest of all the fruits of the Spirit, Love.

It is my aim in this series of Amulree Paperbacks to write popularly on the most profound of subjects; to seek to convey, in comprehensible language, the riches of the great truths and qualities of the Christian faith. To do this involves, on my part, an effort to understand (to use a phrase of Thomas Hardy I made into a chapter heading in *A Day at a Time* Part I, Amulree Paperback No. 2), the "deep-down things" of the spiritual life and the ways in which the Spirit works in our human nature, so that I may be able to go on to convey my understanding of the deep roots of the spiritual life in thoughts, ideas and words which, I hope, everyone can comprehend. I know that I do not always achieve this, but I see it as part of *my* ministry to attempt this task. This book is therefore not one intended for academic purposes but is designed as a pastoral and devotional aid. In other words I want to reflect *with* the reader on the great theme of love and, as a result of that process, to reach the end of this short book hoping that you, the reader, *feels* as well as intellectually understands what love means in its New Testament sense.

I hope to achieve this aim through reflection on St. Paul's great Hymn of Love in the thirteenth chapter of his first letter to the Corinthians. That has been done before! Indeed only last year (1980), Hodder & Stoughton published a new edition of the classic exposition, the most widely read ever of all such expositions, *The Greatest Thing in the World* by Henry Drummond. It was my privilege to be asked to write an Afterword on Henry Drummond for that edition. The material on which I have, however, drawn for *LOVE, the Word that heals* was written for *British Weekly* some time before I had to look more closely at Drummond's impromptu exposition of I Corinthians 13 on the lawn of a Kent garden when the great evangelist Dwight L. Moody (of Moody and Sankey fame) felt too exhausted after much preaching and speaking to address the guests gathered to hear him. He called on his young friend and colleague, Henry Drummond, to undertake the task for him. Thus was born *The Greatest Thing in the World,* a spiritual classic that will endure for all time. I have rather made my own humble approach to the chapter and sought to expand my own material from that series in *British Weekly.* In doing this, I have found the translation of my honoured friend, the late William Barclay, helpful and stimulating. I have therefore, with permission, had I Corinthians 13 in the Barclay version printed at the outset of my reflections alongside the *Authorised Version.* I am grateful to the publisher (Collins) for allowing me the use of the text from Volume II The Letters and the Revelation, of *The New Testament, a new translation* by William Barclay (1969).

"Love is the heartbeat of God." So runs the first statement I make in the entry for January 1 in *A Day at a Time* (Part II, Amulree Paperback No. 3). To reflect on love is to reflect on the very essence of God for God *is* love (I John 4:8). It is no surprise then that the Gospel is summed up so profoundly in terms of *love* — the "eternal triangle" (as I called it in *Creative Silence*) of the love that flows first from God to us and to our neighbour, from us and our neighbour to God, and between our neighbour and us. Only when the three points in the triangle are linked together by the love that flows in all directions is God's will fully expressed and his way truly represented.

So love *is* of God (I John 4:7). No wonder the "more excellent way" (I Corinthians 12:31) or, as the *New English Bible* puts it, "the best way of all" *is* love.

In the text, Biblical quotations are normally from the *Authorised Version (AV)*. If not, the version used will be indicated as *NEB (New English Bible), WB* (William Barclay's translation), *Jerusalem Bible* (Darton, Longman and Todd), *JBP* (J. B. Phillips' *New Testament in Modern English:* Blés). I have not entered into any discussion of the relative merits of the words "charity" and "love". "Charity" from the *Authorised Version* has become "love" in so many of the versions. I simply follow that lead.

I acknowledge gratefully again the co-operation of David Coomes, Editor of *British Weekly* (146 Queen Victoria Street, London EC4) in giving me permission to draw on material first published in that journal. It is owned by Christian Weekly Newspapers. I also acknowledge the help and co-operation of Eve Russell, Managing Director of Arthur James of Evesham, my publishers, in making the publication of this book possible. Once again, I am in debt to my friend, Arthur Ingham, for the cover design and to Jillian Tallon for typing and re-typing my manuscript. I am deeply grateful for her careful and caring help.

DENIS DUNCAN

I Corinthians 13 in William Barclay's translation of
the New Testament

Even if I could speak the languages of men and angels,
    if I am without love,
I am no better than a clanging gong
    or a clashing cymbal.
Even if I have the gift of prophecy,
even if I understand all the secrets
    which only the initiates know;
even if I am wise with all knowledge;
even if I have faith so complete
    that it can move mountains,
    if I am without love,
there is no value in my life.
Even if I dole out everything I possess,
even if I welcome a martyr's death in the flames,
    if I am without love,
it is all no good to me.

Love is patient with people; love is kind.
There is no envy in love;
    there are no proud claims;
    there is no conceit.
Love never does the graceless thing;
    never insists on its rights,
    never irritably loses its temper;
    never nurses its wrath to keep it warm.
Love finds nothing to be glad about
    when someone goes wrong,
    but is glad when truth is glad.
Love can stand any kind of treatment;
    love's first instinct is to believe in people;
    love never regards anyone or anything as hopeless;
    nothing can happen that can break love's spirit.

Love lasts for ever.
 Whatever prophecies there may be,
  they will some day be ended;
 whatever utterances of ecstasy there may be,
  they will some day be silenced;
 whatever knowledge there may be,
  it will some day pass away.
We have but fragments of knowledge
 and glimpses of prophetic insight;
but when the complete will come,
 the fragmentary will be ended.

When I was a child,
 I had a child's speech;
 I had a child's mind;
 I had a child's thoughts.
But, when I became a man,
 I put away childish things.
Now we see bewildering shadows in a mirror,
 but then we shall see face to face;
now I know a fragment of the truth,
 but then I will know as completely as I am known.
The truth is that these three things last for ever —
 faith, hope, love —
 and the greatest of them is love.

I Corinthians 13 in the Authorised Version of the Bible

Though I speak with the tongues of men and of angels,
and have not charity, I am become as sounding brass, or
a tinkling cymbal.

And though I have the gift of prophecy, and understand
all mysteries, and all knowledge; and though I have all
faith, so that I could remove mountains, and have not
charity, I am nothing.

And though I bestow all my goods to feed the poor, and
though I give my body to be burned, and have not
charity, it profiteth me nothing.

Charity suffereth long, and is kind; charity envieth
not; charity vaunteth not itself, is not puffed up.

Doth not behave itself unseemly, seeketh not her own,
is not easily provoked, thinketh no evil;

Rejoiceth not in iniquity, but rejoiceth in the truth;

Beareth all things, believeth all things, hopeth all things,
endureth all things.

Charity never faileth: but whether there be prophecies, they
shall fail; whether there be tongues, they shall cease;
whether there be knowledge, it shall vanish away.

For we know in part, and we prophesy in part.

But when that which is perfect is come, then that which is in
part shall be done away.

When I was a child, I spake as a child, I understood
as a child, I thought as a child: but when I became a
man, I put away childish things.

For now we see through a glass, darkly; but then face
to face: now I know in part; but then shall I know even
as also I am known.

And now abideth faith, hope, charity, these three; but
the greatest of these is charity.

CONTENTS

PREFACE — LOVE, the Word that heals

Part I

Chapter		Page
1	The Primacy of Love	1
2	The Love that is patient	6
3	The Love that is kind	10
4	The Love that knows no envy	14
5	The Love that is truly humble	19
6	The Love that does no graceless thing	23
7	The Love that does not seek its own	26
8	The Love that is not easily provoked	30
9	The Love that thinks no evil	33
10	The Love that rejoices in the truth	36
11	The Love that bears, believes, hopes, endures	40
12	The Love that lasts for ever	53
13	Listen to Love	56
14	Put Love first	59

Part II

15	The Healing Word	63
16	Looking to Jesus	67
17	The Divine Empathy	72
18	The Divine Compassion	77
19	Healing Distance	79
20	The Indwelling Christ	84

Part III

21	Forgiveness	91
22	Redemption	98
23	Reconciliation	103
24	The Paraclete	108
25	The Benediction	112

An Appendix

Cover design by Arthur Ingham

Part I

LOVE

Chapter 1

The Primacy of Love

"Love is the keystone of the arch that joins the soul to God." So wrote my friend and colleague, Martin Israel, in his book *Summons to Life**. It is on that level, with that estimate of the primacy of love, that we approach the theme of Paul's great Hymn of Love.

It is no wonder that, wherever the Gospel is proclaimed and wherever Christians gather to worship, "I Corinthians 13" is known and loved, for St Paul, a man of many parts, has in this hymn touched, with extraordinary understanding, sensitivity and spiritual depth, the very essence of the Christian Gospel. That this man who "began to persecute this (Christian) movement to the death, arresting its followers, men and women alike, and putting them in chains" (Acts 22:4, *NEB*); who "once thought it my duty to work actively against the name of Jesus of Nazareth . . . who imprisoned many of God's people . . . and when they were condemned to death, my vote was cast against them"; who "tried by repeated punishment to make them renounce their faith" and whose "fury rose to such a pitch" that he "extended my (his) persecution to foreign cities" (Acts 26:10-11, *NEB*); that such a man could be so transformed and inwardly renewed that he could see, touch and handle with such profound spiritual delicacy, the concept of the divine love in its very essence, offers the ultimate testimony to the miracle of grace to which he spent the rest of his life bearing witness. If we can follow St Paul to the heights of his vision of the nature of love, we can draw as near to the heart of God as human beings ever can. Preacher, prophet, priest and poet, those many parts of Paul, seem to unite to proclaim, once and for all, the nature of that love which is divine and which excels all human loves.

As is widely known, we have a problem in our English

---

* *published in hardback by Hodder & Stoughton, London, and in paperback by Mowbrays, London.*

language in that the word "love" has to be used to cover four Greek words. There is the word *eros* which is used mostly in the context of human love, "love between the sexes" as William Barclay describes it in his *New Testament Words* (SCM Press). There is *storge* which means family affection, the love of a people for their monarch, etc. There is *philia*, the love and affection that friendship represents, for example the disciple whom Jesus loved (John 20:2) or Jesus' love for Lazarus (John 11:3, 36). There is *agape*, the word used greatly in the New Testament for Christian love because it involves the whole person. Christian love is all-embracing; it is, William Barclay tells us, "a deliberate principle of the mind and a deliberate conquest and achievement of the will. It is in part the power to love the unlovable . . . It takes all of a man to achieve Christian love: it takes not only his heart: it takes his mind and his will as well" *(New Testament Words,* pp. 21-22).

It is this *agape,* this Christian love, which is the basis of the "eternal triangle" to which I have referred in the preface. Love is the foundation of our relationship to God for he *first* loved us and calls out our response in love. Love is the rock on which human relationships are built. Love means "treating men as God treats them" *(op. cit.,* page 23).

I Corinthians 13 is an exposition of love in that New Testament sense. It "joins the soul to God" because God has, in the great divine initiative, sought out our souls in their need. It binds human beings together — with "cords of love." It is the fount and foundation of Christian life and service. Love is of God, for God *is* love.

In all our reflecting on this divine love, it is important to remember the particular sense in which we are using the word "love" in this book. So often the word has been prostituted in the sense that parts of the meaning of "love" have been taken as the whole of its meaning. So one or two aspects of love have been made to look as if they actually were love.

Romantic love, erotic love, "physical" love are spoken of today as if any one of them, or all three together for that matter, are the same as *agape* or love in the New Testament sense. So love is trivialised, misunderstood, misrepresented, commercialised and plagiarised by the less commendable contributors to the media. It loses its real meaning as the basis on which wholeness in "body, soul, mind and spirit", wholeness in the "physical, mental, emotional and spiritual" areas of us all, depends. Love *is* the Word that heals provided only that we mean the divine love in all its fullness. Anything less than that way of understanding Christian love is short of the understanding Paul has of *agape*. It is only when we have *agape* in all its wholeness and profundity as God's love in Christ flowing out to humanity and creating responses to it that we have "the Word that heals."

Paul's Hymn of Love begins with a statement about the *primacy of love,* which is the clue to our understanding of the spiritual life. Without love, no matter what I do, I am nothing. Magnificence of utterance without love is no more than empty noise — sounding gong, clanging cymbal. Deep intuition, prophetic insight and monumental faith are nothing if not rooted and grounded in love. Philanthropy and even martyrdom, if the motive of love is missing, are pointless and unproductive. Nothing is of use if love is lacking. Nothing.

The impact of that statement is shattering in relation to so much that we do. The implications of it reach to the very depths of our being. But it is in fact the reality that Paul himself came to know and it is the truth that Jesus specifically expressed. Paul, in his personal defence of his apostleship in his letter to the Philippians (chapter 3, *NEB*), records that "his pride is in Christ" and he "puts no confidence in things external." He goes on: "If anyone thinks to base his claims on externals, I could make a stronger case for myself — circumcised on my eighth day, Israelite by race, of the tribe of Benjamin, a Hebrew born and bred; in my attitude to the law, a Pharisee; in pious zeal, a persecutor of the church; in legal rectitude, faultless. But all such assets I have written off because of Christ. I would say more: I count everything sheer loss, because all is far outweighed by the gain of knowing Christ Jesus my Lord, for whose sake I did in fact lose everything. I count it so much garbage, for the sake of gaining Christ and finding myself incorporate in him, with no righteousness of my own, no legal rectitude, but the righteousness which comes from faith in Christ, given by God in response to faith. All I care for is to know Christ . . ." The Hymn of Love is not a lyrical outburst totally unrelated to reality. It is an expression of the most fundamental convictions Paul had about the uselessness of anything which lacks love.

Paul's insistence on the centrality of Christ and the love, divine and human which relates to him, is borne out very clearly in the Gospel record. The story of "the woman of bad reputation" (William Barclay) who came to the house of Simon the Pharisee (Luke 7:36—50) and drenched his feet with her tears in order to wipe them with her hair is an example of the very strong line Jesus took on the question of formal, as against sincere, love, for it was the technically righteous Pharisee who received what can only be described as a verbal lashing from Jesus on his lack of love, care and sensitivity. Salt was poured into his wounds by the Master's acceptance and warm commendation of the sincere love of that "immoral" woman, a love spontaneously expressed and tenderly offered. Without love, Simon was nothing — despite his position, reputation and religion. Given love, other things can be accepted and understood. To "love much" in sincerity is to be so much nearer the heartbeat of God than to love "officially" but without warmth.

The primacy of love is woven into the very fabric of life in the Spirit. Loving relationships must characterise all that such life means. Between myself and God there is a mystical union to be discovered (realising that the initiator of the relationship is always God for "we love him because he first loved us") just as there is the same union to be formed between God and my neighbour. That is the "vertical" in the symbol of the Cross. But if there is no "horizontal" (the arms outstretched) relationship between my neighbour and me, a relationship which the "vertical" relationship makes essential, that mystical union becomes irrelevant and indeed impossible. It is no accident that the primacy of love is expressed in the symbol of the Cross, the place where "vertical" and "horizontal" meet.

Life in the Spirit, the love-dominated life, is both a "one-to-one" relationship with God and its "communal" expression in the life of the world. There is, in the end, no gap or void between "individual" and "social" Christianity. The love-filled life is a combination of both. If we seek mystical relationship without community involvement, we shall have, if we have anything, an empty piety. If we are socially conscious but in such a way as to obliterate faith, we shall do good social work, but it will not be life in the Spirit. The Cross that draws personal and social Christianity together is the most effective reminder possible of the primacy of love.

Chapter 2

The Love that is patient

It is a mistake to try to break love up into the elements that compose it. As is the case with magic, analysis only succeeds in destroying the concept altogether. But we can look at love with humility and in awe, and glimpse some of the qualities that are inherent in it. Here, in one situation, one aspect reveals itself, there in another, we sense a different characteristic of love. I Corinthians 13 is Paul's inspired effort to catch and record the different faces of love.

I say "inspired effort." It was indeed this. I feel I can best serve the seeker after a greater degree of true love by resisting the temptation to offer one's own (to use Henry Drummond's phrase) "analysis of love." Paul has touched the greatest possible heights in his ecstatic essay on "the best way of all." If ecstasy is standing outside oneself under the impact of the divine Spirit, and so, as I see it, being pushed to heights of awareness beyond the normal, then the Hymn of Love is surely a product of ecstasy. I shall benefit readers best by taking the Pauline insight into the nature of love as my "text" and offering extended comment on it, from where we stand in our own times and circumstances.

"Love is patient" Paul says.

Patience, proverbially, is a virtue, but it is a virtue seen in different ways by different people. It will appear to some as the capacity to cope, in calm consideration, over a long period, with the contentious, the confusing, the trying and the "difficult." It speaks of some degree of inner consistency, of solidity, of commitment under pressure. It is a quality that, on the whole, is untypical of our hurried, harassed world. Lack of patience leads to unpleasantness, anger, frustration and division and produces broken relationships and unreconciled situations.

There are those who are ever ready to criticise the over-patient and the long-suffering for putting up with more than they should tolerate. Modern psychological theory often places great emphasis on the need to show one's anger and acknowledge one's impatience. My own belief is that there is too little patience in the world today and too much impatience and I have nothing but admiration for those who, with infinite patience, help, teach and care for the mentally handicapped, the physically disabled, the socially deprived and the psychologically disturbed. Love is — or ought to be — patient.

But in the New Testament conception of the love that is "patient," there is more to it than that. We need to move to a deeper dimension of patience, one that is rooted in the belief often recognised in the Old Testament and incarnate in the New Testament, that God, being love, is willing to wait, at a cost, for the loving response he seeks.

The word "patient" is, by derivation, linked with suffering. The Bible extends this link by moving to the concept of (as the *Authorised Version* renders it) "long-suffering." So the patience of God is expressed dramatically in the Pauline phrase (verse 4) on which we are reflecting here: Love "suffers long . . ."

The Greek word for long-suffering is *makrothumia*. It means "a long holding out of the mind before it gives room to action or passion . . ." (French, *Synonyms of the New Testament*). It witnesses to the "steadfast spirit which will never give in" (William Barclay, *New Testament Words*). It is used by Paul in his letter to the Romans (Chapter 2, verse 4) to describe the "goodness and forbearance and long-suffering" of God. Having listed the appalling corruption described so vividly in Chapter 1 of the letter (see especially verse 18 to the end of the chapter), Paul points to the divine patience which has refrained from the judgement which would be appropriate to such wickedness, but has rather, in

loving forbearance, redeemed those involved in such
degradation. "Do you think lightly of (God's) wealth of
kindness, of tolerance and of patience?" (Romans 2:4 *NEB*).
Again in Romans Chapter 9, verse 22 (*WB*), Paul talks of
God's right to demonstrate his wrath, but "in spite of that, he
bore very patiently with the men and women he had created,
men and women who deserved nothing but his wrath and who
were fit for nothing but destruction." Paul even sees himself
as a classic example of the way the divine patience is shown.
"But I received mercy" he writes to Timothy (I Timothy 1:16,
WB) "and it was for this reason. Christ Jesus wanted me to
be the first in whom he might display all his patience for
everyone to see, because he wanted me to be an example of
those who were going to believe in him and so find eternal
life."

Throughout the New Testament, it is made clear that the
disciple must be like his Master; that if there is a divine
attitude to life, that attitude must be reflected in the disciple's
attitude. Inevitably then, patience being at the very heart of
God's attitude to us, we must also have patience towards
other people. It is no surprise to find long-suffering or
patience listed in Paul's fruits of the Spirit (Galatians 5:22).
Christians must be as patient and long-suffering as possible
with others, because God suffers long in love for his people.

That example from "the harvest of the Spirit" is important
for it emphasises the wholly creative and positive aspects of
patience. In popular parlance, long-suffering has a negative
sound. In fact it is in no way negative as a description of the
love of God. The patience of God — as I said earlier — is
positive in purpose. It is slow to react in passion and action
(as French defined the word above) because such a reaction
might defeat all that God seeks — the redemption of the
sinner, the return of the prodigal, the rehabilitation of the
broken. Without exception, every demonstration of God's
patient long-suffering is intended to win the wanderer's love
and gently lead to home. In other words, love is of a kind that
goes to "the ultimate", "any lengths" to offer forgiveness and

the opportunity of new life. Such life-giving love implies, as I said in my last chapter, cost and pain. "God *so* loved the world that he gave . . ." The Cross remains the symbol of "the best way of all", the way of patient love.

It is to this kind of love, so easy to write about in theory, so hard to live out in practice, that the disciple is called. It is not of the nature of humanity to "suffer long." We can be so impatient with the persistent, so irritated with the perpetual invader of our privacy, so provoked by the critic, so little able to suffer for long the difficult, the deceiving and the dull. Yet the message of the Hymn of Love is clear. The attitude of God to his people has to be our attitude to others. We must, in every situation, remember that the divine purpose is always to redeem, to recover, and to renew. We dare not then lose sight of our own function within the body of Christ. The sharp action, the over-reaction may, in human terms, be understandable, but it is not the way of love, for Love is *always* patient. Love truly "suffers long."

Chapter 3

The Love that is kind

"Be kind to each other." So Paul wrote in his letter to the church at Ephesus (4:32 *JBP*). The *New English Bible* translates that word "kind" as "generous." That is helpful, for "kindness" is essentially a quality that has deeply embedded in it *the desire to bless someone with good.*

If you look up your dictionary, you will almost certainly find that this element — the disposition to do good to another — is central to the concept of kindness. Kindness — in terms of this desire to bless — is conceived in the womb of compassion. Kindness involves understanding. Kindness longs for all to be "truly well" and is prepared to do what it can to bring about well-being.

Love, Paul tells us then, is "kind." There is a divine kindness at the heart of God, for God is love (I John 4:8) and love is of God (I John 4:7). God is disposed to do us good. God seeks not to condemn, but to save. God's only desire is our blessing; his only motive is our redemption, salvation, wholeness, well-being. So the God whose wonder Paul is praising, is one who understands human fallibility and makes allowance for human weakness. It is evidence of the reality of Jesus' being "one with the Father" that he shows the divine kindness incarnate when he is, as he seemed not infrequently to be, "moved with compassion." So the divine love flows out to people in need, indeed to humanity as a whole, for it is the divine will, Paul tells us in his first letter to Timothy (2:4), that "all men should find salvation and come to a knowledge of the truth."

It is for this very reason that God is "with us" (Matthew 1:23), with us not only in the sense of being beside us and among us, but with us in the more colloquial sense of being "for" us. He is disposed to do us good. There is indeed a "divine kindness" at the heart of the God who is love. There must then be human kindness in the heart of human beings who claim the description "disciples."

The translations vary in how closely they link the divine patience and the divine kindness. The *Authorised Version* keeps the two concepts closely together in its rendering: "Love suffers long and is kind." J. B. Phillips and the *Jerusalem Bible* — and others — make the link real too. If the divine patience has, as its essential element, the quality of "long-suffering" (as we saw in our last chapter), then the word "compassion" becomes the central concept in kindness. The divine kindness is love expressed in compassion for our ultimate good. The kindness then that we must show consists of these same elements. We are committed to compassionate concern for others in the hope and belief that what we are offering, if accepted, will be for their true good. Unkindness is, manifestly, the exact opposite of this.

J. B. Phillips, in his *Letters to Young Churches,* makes his own effort to focus our attention on the creative aspect of kindness. His translation of the words "Love is kind" is expressed like this: "Love looks for a way of being constructive." Kindness is never possessiveness (I shall return to this point later), nor is it action of a kind that denies freedom to personality. Kindness is never expressed in "take-over." It is an offering, out of compassion, of that which we *can* give, and which we hope, if it is accepted, will add blessing to another human soul.

The element that is compassion and so is in kindness is important. Kindness relates to the creative contribution we can make to the life of another human being. It has an "enabling" quality that helps bring out the good and the beautiful in the one chosen to be its recipient. It reflects the feelings of compassion and goodwill that are at the heart of the divine love which has only one aim — to do us good.

Let us return now to the practical point I raised above when I said "Kindness is never possessiveness", for it is one of the areas of life in which a proper understanding of the motivation of true kindness is important.

"Love does not dominate: it cultivates" says a poster on my study wall. How true this is of the divine kindness! How true it must be of ours! But sadly life illustrates only too often the disastrous effects of over-possessiveness in family life and human relationships. So often we meet the victims of uncontrolled "kindness," that is the determination to "do someone good" that leaves them no room to develop, gives them no "space" of their own to occupy, allows them no possible opportunity to evolve a proper independence and freedom. And so there are people who, smothered by over-possessive parents and given no areas of decision, are dominated all their lives by authoritarian fathers who *decide* what is good and invalid mothers who subtly but unflinchingly close the door on their only daughter's marriage in the name of caring. How often in life we find illness used as a weapon of manipulation in situations where demanding parents will not let their family go. The counselling rooms of the country, be it here or elsewhere, are occupied by middle-aged people who have been totally caught up in dependent relationships from which they are simply not able — for many "good" reasons when taken at the conscious level — to detach themselves. It is wise to remember C. Day Lewis' words

> Selfhood begins with a walking away
> and love is proved in the letting go.

Love as kindness is never a smothering process. It is a cultivating one. It never aims to bind, only to liberate. It is not offered as an order to be obeyed, but as a gift to be received. Kindness implies freedom on both sides of the relationship. And where is the model for this whole concept of relationship but in that relationship we have, in Christ, to God? Jesus watched the rich young ruler walk away (Matthew 19:16–22). He did it sadly, but he did it in the true spirit of love. You cannot, and must not, browbeat people into the Kingdom. You dare not manipulate the Holy Spirit (as Simon Magus found out so traumatically in his confrontation with

Peter on the subject, as recorded in Acts 8). The prodigal son was free to go. The father would want and yearn and pray, but never go and fetch. So the divine kindness is revealed. Salvation is not a magic potion but a gift of grace, to be received or rejected. Our human kindness must always be offered on the pattern shown so clearly in the New Testament. It can be taken or left, received or rejected, but never forced on anyone.

In this divine way, "be kind to each other."

Chapter 4

The Love that knows no envy

Envy is the antithesis of Christian love. It is linked in the New Testament with strife, division, hatred, even murder and these are all denials of love. We find these associations in such passages as Matthew 27:18 where we read that Pilate "knew that for *envy* they had delivered" Jesus; Romans 1:29 where we find "full of envy" in the list of "ungodly", "unrighteous" attitudes and happenings typical of the times at the beginning of the letter to the Romans to which I have already referred; Romans 13:13, "Let us walk ... not ... in strife and envying;" Galatians 5:19–21, "the works of the flesh are ... envyings;" James 3:16 "where envying and strife is, there is confusion and every evil work" etc., etc.

Envy is "an attribute of the Devil" according to Bacon in his essay on "Envy." Through it relationships are endangered, poisoned and often, in the end, broken — as they were, for example, between Cain and Abel, Jacob and Esau, Joseph and his brothers, King Saul and David, and in the relationship of "elder brother" and "prodigal son." It was not wholly absent even at such high levels of sanctification as those represented by Peter and Paul! Envy is indeed a deadly sin. It is no part of the way of love.

The *Authorised Version* and the *New English Bible* are in accord in this context. The *Jerusalem Bible* introduces the word "jealous" in its version while J. B. Phillips interprets the fault as "possessiveness." The essential element in the word "envy" is certainly the idea of "grudging", so the dictionary definition concentrates on that element and describes it as "grudging ill-will at another's superiority", or, it might be, over another's possessions. It is certainly usual to find envy at work where both position and possessions are involved. Jealousy (the choice of the *Jerusalem Bible*) adds an element not always present in envy but certainly related to it — the feeling of "suspicious apprehension" summed up in the modern, if jargon, word "threatened."

Whichever complex of ideas we use, the end result is the same. There is no place for envy in the New Testament view of "the best way of all", the way of love. If, moreover, as we have said, "God is love" and "love is of God", thus making love the fundamental divine attribute and the quality the disciple must express too, it is obvious that divine love "envies not." The God who *is* love does not envy and his disciples too should not be envious. The God who *is* love cannot envy anyone, and the disciple must guard against the possibility of the creeping spiritual paralysis that that fault brings. After all, envy was part of the primal sin in the Garden of Eden. It was the desire to be as God and know everything that led to the downfall of humanity. Envy must be resisted with every measure of grace available.

That is the theory — the realities of life are different! For all of us, feelings of envy are real at some time or another. However deeply we feel the miracle of grace has affected us, we are still but learners on the way to sanctification. We are all too familiar with the feeling of envy however much we hate that deadly sin.

I referred above to the part envy played in problems involving Peter and Paul. The issues were, intellectually, described in terms of the relationship between Jew and Gentile, as matters concerning circumcision, etc., but underneath those genuine issues there were feelings too, some personal, some "collective", coming from the different positions occupied by the two leaders of the Christian church. Some consciousness of the dangers of envy can also be seen in the self-strictures of Paul on several occasions (for example in II Corinthians 12 where Paul confesses the presence of his "thorn in the flesh" to keep him from being "too uplifted"). There is also a hint of the problems of position and the envy that comes with false ambition, in the rival claims, referred to in I Corinthians chapter 1, where there was envious contention audible in rallying cries such as "I am of Paul", "I am of Cephas", "I am of Apollos". Where there is envy, there comes division. Friendships can be soured, negative feelings can build up to sabotage sanctification and stunt the growth of Christian love. Unchecked, envy can disrupt creative development, destroy inner peace and defeat the evolution of that inner security by which we live — and love.

The same is true in public matters. Envy has manifestly contributed to wars and fighting. The desire for territory and the power that possession of it is believed to bring, has led to aggression and invasion. Envy is behind racial intolerance and prejudice, political manipulation and manoeuvre. Especially has this been so in an essentially materialistic age when "to have" is so important in terms of power, personal prestige and position.

It is sad, but realistic, to have to add that church life too is familiar with this fault. All too often envy makes its presence felt both in the ecclesiastical corridors of power and in the local congregation. Indeed family feuds are sometimes taken into the life of the local church and striving for positions of office is an expression of envious conflicts that belong outside the church and have no right to be projected into it. The text "Love envies not" ought to be displayed in many a suite of church buildings, in its committee rooms and in its council chambers. We have all seen the presence of envy in the church at parish, national and international level.

"There is no fear in love" John tells us in his first Letter (I John 4:18). Fear and love just cannot live together. Envy has much of fear in it, fear of failure, fear of lack of power, fear of domination. If such envy is a potent presence within us, it is essential that we should face up to and understand its presence in our lives. The roots of it may be in unhappy childhood experience. The power it has within us may come from our being threatened by another's ability, achievement, experience, knowledge. Awareness of these feelings should prompt us to honesty with ourselves before God or, if we cannot do it in prayer alone, to seek help through a relationship of trust that compels us to face up to the feelings in us. Only honest grappling with the feelings that so easily beset us, before God or with another who can help us to feel in the presence of God, can allow "wave upon wave of grace"* to flow through our being, illuminating our feelings of envy and, possibly, the reasons for them and enabling us to accept them, acknowledge them and have them redeemed. Thus grace will attack the sin of envy and love will take the place of the fear it generates.

Modern psychology, as I have said at greater length in my *Creative Silence,* has helped us to understand the presence of "unconscious" factors in our make-up both "personal" and "collective" (in the Jungian sense of the "collective unconscious").** Feelings of envy are often deeply embedded within us because of the way we have repressed what we could not cope with in earlier years. But repression, that is the dismissal of what we cannot tolerate, to the unconscious, does not mean those feelings do not exist any more. They do, but we do not know they are there and active and can be touched off by some event, situation or person. When these feelings of envy begin to distort our rational judgements or spoil our relationships, we can feel guilty and sick at heart, knowing consciously that we should be loving, but aware that we are consumed with envy. As a result of that ambivalence, we become thoroughly miserable through the guilt too! The experience is common to all sensitive to the Christian ideal, and no one expressed it more traumatically than Paul in Romans chapter 7, when he cried out in desperation over the conflict between good and evil, within him. It is part of the Christian struggle to wrestle with these things. "Love envies not", but we do! We need the sanctifying grace that will enable us to see our need, acknowledge our "fault", accept ourselves with love as we are and offer ourselves to the redeeming grace. Fear and love, envy and love, cannot live together. Let love triumph! Let envy go, for "love envies not"!

Before I complete our reflection on this theme, it is necessary to insert a reminder that, while envy is wrong

*John 1:16 (WB)
**See Appendix also on this matter.

because of its "grudging" element, there is a legitimate longing, a proper yearning whereby we express our deep wish for profoundly desirable achievement, especially of a spiritual kind, attained by others. But this proper longing has nothing in common with the envious feelings I have been describing. Seeking and longing after that which is good and lovely and earnestly desiring to have it is in no way related to the envy of the sin-full kind. It is a desire to have, to be, to reach out in a way that recalls Paul's great words: "I press toward the mark for the prize of the high calling of God in Christ Jesus" (Philippians 3:14). Such reaching out for what others have in humble faith, can only be good. It is very far from the grudging envy, the deadly sin I have been describing. In that reaching out love envies not. It is that other wholly negative attitude that has no place in "the best way of all."

Chapter 5

The Love that is truly humble

The translations may vary and the descriptive phrases differ in detail, but the ringing truth conveyed by St Paul in this last ɪ art of verse 4 is in no doubt at all. Love is not boastful nor is it conceited. It does not set out, anxiously, to impress others. It has no inflated idea of its own importance. Love "vaunteth not itself: is not puffed up." Love always presents herself in the garments of humility, for humility is of the essence of the loveliness and the loving-ness of love.

Humility all too often has been given a self-effacing, self-deprecating sound and so has been associated with weakness. The wringing hands of the so-called "humble", cringing before superior power, creeping surreptitiously onwards in the pursuit of position in feigned self-abasement, crawling ignominiously into acceptance with dishonour, has even, in such extreme images, been linked with humility. Whatever history this association of ideas has — and it did represent concepts of humility in the thought of ancient Greece and Rome — it has nothing whatever to do with Christian humility.

It is, once again, to that concept which is so fundamental to I Corinthians 13, that we must go. Love is *of God*. God *is* love. The grace of humility that we must acquire is rooted in the divine love. The garment of humility we must wear is based on the divine pattern of humility expressed uniquely in Jesus Christ.

That humility is set out for us in another magnificent passage from one of Paul's letters, the letter to the church at Philippi. I cannot do other than quote this amazing section (chapter 2, verses 5–11, *WB*):

"He shared the very being of God, but he did not regard his equality to God as a thing to be clutched to himself. So far from that, he emptied himself, and really and truly became a servant, and was made for a time exactly like man. In a human form that all could see, he accepted such a depth of humiliation that he was prepared to die, and to die on a cross. That is why God has given him the highest place, and has conferred on him the name that is greater than any name, so that, at the name of Jesus, every creature in heaven, and on earth, and beneath the earth should kneel in reverence and submission, and so that everything which has a voice should openly declare that Jesus Christ is Lord and thus bring glory to God the Father."

Humility is not a denial of our worth. It is a recognition of it. As the *New English Bible* renders that passage, it is stressed that "the divine nature was his from the first." He did not lack worth; he possessed it uniquely. Humility arises specifically where personal value is recognised and acknowledged but is not made a matter of boasting and conceit. It is precisely because Christ "shared the very being of God" yet "did not regard his equality to be clutched to himself" that his true humility is so movingly splendid. He voluntarily and freely and deliberately "humbled" himself and in obedience accepted death — even death on a cross.

It is this attitude which is the essence of humility in the Christian conception as against ordinary dictionary definitions of the word "humility." It is this which is the strength of Christian humility. There is no weakness in it. So it was possible for Christ to perform acts of humility — washing the disciples' feet for example — without losing true greatness. On the contrary, humility of this depth enhances and honours. "That is *why* God has given him the highest place." Humility ends in growth, greatness and grandeur.

St Paul's plea to the Philippians to express true humility is rooted and grounded in the divine humility, demonstrated in Christ. "Try to have the same attitude to life as Jesus had" he writes (William Barclay's version, chapter 2, verses 1–4). "If there is such a thing as Christian encouragement, if there is such a thing as love's comforting power, if you and I are really sharing in the partnership which only the Holy Spirit can make possible, if you really wish to show me a heartfelt sympathy which is like the mercy of God, make my joy complete by being in perfect harmony of mind, by joining in a common love for God and for each other, by sharing in a common life, by taking every decision in unity of mind, by never acting from motives of competitive rivalry or in the conceited desire for empty prestige. If you want to make my joy complete, instead of that each of you must humbly think the other better than himself; each of you must concentrate, not on his own interest, but on the interests of others also."

Humility is a mark of true Christian love. It will always "increase" us rather than "decrease" us if we can find the secret of it. It is when we set out to boast and be conceited that we lose spiritual stature for love "vaunteth not itself, is not puffed up." It is when we clothe ourselves in the garments of humility that we truly grow in the inner depths of our being.

Paradoxically, that is a growth that we can never plan, yet it follows as day does the night, in the heart and soul of the truly humble. Humility is an integral part of "the best way of all." Listen to love — and find true humility.

The saints of God have always demonstrated this great Christian quality. Indeed its absence or presence is a test of true Christian quality. Arrogance is wholly foreign to Christian character. There is no place for the exalted claims of the arrogant in a faith that has the divine humility at the centre of it. "To give and not to count the cost;" to accept participation in the human lot instead of abusing the divine power available to him and to share our suffering, pain and temptation as a demonstration of the true humanity of the Son of God; to empty himself — these are the stones in the edifice of love of which Christ himself was the corner-stone. It is impossible, given the acted parable of the divine nature itself, to represent Christ unless there is, in the representative, a true humility.

Perhaps this is the hardest part of the Gospel to accept, yet it is the essential part. "Nothing in my hands I bring: simply to Thy Cross I cling." Of ourselves we can do nothing. Through "the grace which is sufficient for us", "all things become possible." "It is the Lord's doing and it is marvellous in our eyes." How can the disciple, conscious of the divine initiative and the totality of God's giving to the world, be other than moved to humility?

So when humility is learned, there can be true gladness. It is a sign that "the best way of all", the way of love, is truly being learned.

Chapter 6

The Love that does no graceless thing

Love "does not behave itself unseemly." So runs verse 5. It would be interesting to know just what that phrase conveys to different people. I suspect that, for most, it has a specifically *moral* "feel" about it. So being translated into those terms, it would read: "Love is not guilty of immoral behaviour."

Let us take that thought a little further. The phrase "immoral behaviour" means, for many a Christian, sexual misbehaviour for it is the case that, in church circles particularly, that area has been associated more than any other part of life with sin. Jesus, on the other hand, consistently drew attention to the much wider and, perhaps really, more serious forms of immoral behaviour — those associated with spiritual pride, envy, intolerance, arrogance, self-righteousness, selfishness, etc. So whatever "unseemly" behaviour is, it is much more than statutory immoral behaviour. *It has something to say about a person's whole attitude to life and to people.*

For the *Authorised Version's* "unseemly", the *New English Bible* uses the word "rude." But that word too is ambiguous. It can mean, in an extended sense, in dictionary definition, "insolent, offensive, insulting", yet its primary meaning is a much more pleasant and acceptable one — simple, unsophisticated and genuine in a primitive kind of way (as we find in the phrase from the Christmas Carol describing the Bethlehem stable as "rude and bare"). I prefer then to go to William Barclay and J. B. Phillips for illumination on these words of Paul. Dr. Phillips' *New Testament in Modern English* interprets the phrase like this: "Love has good manners", bringing an element of courtesy and consideration into the "seemliness" of behaviour, but Dr. Barclay provides for me the most helpful alternative of all by his rendering:

"Love never does the grace-less thing." Unseemly behaviour is behaviour that lacks "grace."

"Grace" is, again, a word that has many shades of meaning. It is an almost indefinable word involving, first and in its "ordinary" sense, elements of charm, refinement and elegance, but in its New Testament sense, there come the very specific meanings of goodwill, favour and undeserved benefit at the hands of a loving God.

It therefore speaks of that which spiritually blesses, uplifts, transforms and renews at the deepest levels of life. Grace reaches down into the very heart of the human struggle and brings grace-full influence to bear on the battle waged in the human soul — as it is in the cosmic universe — between good and evil. Grace contributes through its capacity, as the gift of the Holy Spirit, to renew, re-create, regenerate and spiritually invigorate. That is "good." That which degrades, defiles, diminishes and distorts, damages our spiritual welfare and so belongs to "evil."

"Grace-less-ness" is then the characteristic of everything that pulls down rather than builds up, degrades rather than refines, brings deterioration rather than spiritual improvement. Love can therefore *never* do "the grace-less thing" for all it offers is for our ultimate good. Love can have no connection with attitudes or behaviour that degrade mankind, that take humanity away from the spiritual and the divine, that afflict or influence human beings in a deleterious or a destructive way. So love is always "on the side of the angels" and will never involve itself in behaviour that is conducive to the production of evil of any kind.

All who seek to follow "the best way of all" and "press toward the mark for the prize of the high calling of God in Christ Jesus" by showing the harvest of the Spirit in an increasingly sanctified life, will not willingly behave in an unseemly way. The gracelessness such attitudes or conduct involve is destructive to growth in Christ on the part of an individual. It is, moreover, at the communal level, an equally important factor for all policies that diminish the quality of life are policies which in principle the Christian cannot support. There is a guideline here by which to test out policies of a political, educational, medical or any other kind. Love cannot be a party to the gracelessness that degrades, diminishes or destroys. Pornography, pollution, prejudice in a racial or social context are graceless things. They are not of love. They act against the things that are "good and lovely and of good report" and in so doing damage the quality of life itself.

A similar test must be applied to other public issues — stewardship of the earth's resources, nuclear proliferation, the use of language, abortion, euthanasia, media permissiveness, industrial relations, etc., etc. Is what is being offered, provided, developed, proclaimed an addition to the good which God wills for all his people or does it subtract from it and so, in the process, add to the sum of evil? If the latter is the case, then these are "graceless things" and no part of the healing word of love.

In this apparently simple phrase, we do find something that reaches to the very roots of salvation and spiritual growth as well as ethical discussion. We are dealing with much more than moral peccadilloes, bad manners or social indiscretion. We are dealing in essence with the effect all that we do, or are may have on our own and others' spiritual wholeness. These are the things that are the concern of God. He has made salvation, wholeness, health, possible in Christ, through the Holy Spirit. In the act of conversion, justification, "turn-around", redemption — call it what you will — he has offered the opportunity of "life abundant", true and authentic life. The process of spiritual growth and sanctification goes on from there, enriched by the Spirit, aided by the means of grace, stimulated by prayer. Graceless things delay our growth into the fullness of the stature of our Lord Jesus Christ and hold back our progress in the spiritual life.

With so much at issue that touches the very purpose of life itself, it is clear that love can never, in any circumstances, "do the grace-less thing."

Chapter 7

The Love that does not seek its own

"Love seeketh not her own." Perhaps this is a statement about the nature of our "centre." "Where your treasure is, there will your heart be also" said Jesus when he made a pertinent comment on the way the human mind and heart tend to behave. To have the right "centre" to our being is imperative if we are going to resonate creatively. That right centre can never be *self.* Love is not "selfish" — as the *New English Bible* translates this verse. "Love does not pursue selfish advantage" is J. B. Phillips' version. In other words, love can never be self-centred.

It is worthwhile reflecting on the danger of that self-centredness which is so contrary to the divine pattern of relationship, and on the need for the proper centredness of the self, as a child of God, made in the image of God. It takes us to such themes as balance, perspective and proportion, concepts deeply embedded in the New Testament. "Seek ye first the Kingdom of God, and his righteousness; and all these things shall be added unto you" (Matthew 6:33) is a statement about the right balance between things spiritual and things material. It is about the right priorities. It is about proportion. "The things which are seen are temporal; but the things which are not seen are eternal" (II Corinthians 4:18) is a statement about perspective.

It is worth saying a little more about balance in the context of the faith, because the essence of correct balance is a sound relationship of the parts to the centre. In this context, Jesus was surely the most balanced person ever. He functioned from a calm, strong inner centre and reflected the perfect relationship between the physical, mental, emotional and spiritual aspects of his life. It is interesting that we describe someone who is emotionally or mentally ill or underdeveloped as "unbalanced."

The concept of balance, like the exhortation to be an "ordered" person, sounds dull and unadventurous, but balance and order in a Christian context are far from that. We have sometimes to be fools for Christ's sake! That sounds anything but a discouragement to adventure for it speaks rather of risk of many kinds. But disciples are *disciplined* people. The Holy Spirit is not expressed in disorder, but in order, and we should question whether the Spirit is present, as is often claimed, in situations of disorder, emotional or otherwise. The important and fundamental point is that it is the balanced person who is best suited to take risks. Once again Jesus demonstrated that so exactly. It was because he was so balanced that he had to say and do things that upset "authority", secular or religious. It was the ordered, disciplined man of Nazareth, totally "centred" in faith, hope and love who could accept, as his voluntary mission, the risky road that must lead to crucifixion. The Cross was a *skandalon* to Greeks and Jews — to the former "foolishness", to the latter "a stumbling block", but it was in no sense, when you look at it *sub specie aeternitatis,* from the standpoint of eternity, an act of eccentricity. It was "the power of God unto salvation" and represented the balanced, ordered will of God who risked sending his Son to share in the life of the world.

At the heart of the divine nature there is a love that flows out in compassion to humanity. "God so loved the world that he gave ..." The longing to give is not the product of selfishness or self-centredness. And even if we have to be aware of what we are doing in applying these anthropomorphic words to the Deity, the truth they express is valid. It is God's nature to give rather than to keep. It must be the disciple's nature too, to give and to give out, rather than to hold and to keep. There is no place for the self-centred man or woman in the Christian community.

All this serves to underline the kind of "map" we must have against which we are to live out our lives. I discussed in *Creative Silence* the nature of the map many make for themselves, the one that is based squarely on the "reality" of this world of space and time. We, as Christians must, make our map one which takes account of the reality of spiritual dimensions largely unknown to the life of the world. The perspective from which we see life is conditioned wholly by the choice we make here. What is important in our reflection on the dangers of self-centredness is the choice we are called to make in designing our map. Do we put ourselves at the centre of our world and expect the world to revolve around us, or do we make our lives "God-centred", "Christ-centred"?

If we do place ourselves at the centre of everything, and see life as that in which *our* needs are primary, see the world as one in which *our* needs must be met, see discussion as no more than a way of demonstrating that *our* ways are right, then we are creating a world in which we "seek our own." *We* determine the ends. *We* control and manipulate the means. *We* use people as pawns in *our* game.

To get ourselves into this self-centred position, where we do all we can to forward our own purposes, is to produce a life which is a denial of "the best way of all." For love is not concerned with the manipulation of everything and everyone for *our* use. It is the opposite. It is the outflow of love and compassion in service to others. There is a fundamental difference of direction in the two philosophies of life. The direction we have chosen is crucial to our salvation. The centre we have is critical for our wholeness.

If any evidence is needed of the danger of "off-centre" attitudes and what can follow from such eccentricity (deviating from a true centre) and indeed ego-centricity (the placing of the self at the centre), we need look no further than the book of the Acts of the Apostles where we read of the manipulating of Simon Magus to whom I referred earlier. Here indeed is a sorcerer who sought his own! In Acts 8, we are told he "believed" and had been baptised (verse 13) but that spiritual experience had not really touched his inner self at all for he then asked (verse 20) if he could buy the power of the Holy Spirit. In his self-centredness, he would seek even to manipulate God. (Shades indeed of that primal sin in the Garden of Eden again!) No wonder that other Simon — Peter this time — had to say to him (verse 21): "Thy heart is not right in the sight of God." Here indeed was a balance to be corrected, a perspective to be adjusted, proportion to be evolved.

So I return, with emphasis, to the statements I have made already on the sin of self-centredness. If the disciple is to model himself on the God who is love by nature, then there cannot but be a total rejection of selfishness. It is not the way of divine love to get or to keep, to manipulate or to control. It is the way of God to give.

> Love ever gives
> Forgives
> Outlives
> Ever stands
> With open hands
> And while it lives
> It gives
> For this is love's prerogative
> To give
> And give
> And give

"God so loved the world that he gave ..." (John 3:16). I quoted this above as the statement about the Christian's God that is definitive of his nature. Christ emptied himself (Philippians 2:5–11) — a total self-giving for the sake of all humanity. Because he *first* loved us, we love him (I John 4:19). Our lives must reflect the "givingness" of God. If it is of the very essence of divine love to "flow out" in compassion, then it is of the essence of the disciplined life to flow out too, in love to the world. How can we ever, in such a calling, have a love that "seeks its own?"

Chapter 8

The Love that is not easily provoked

There is an incident in the Gospel which illustrates so clearly this aspect of "the best way of all" that I take you to it immediately. It is in Mark's gospel, chapter 14 verses 53–65 and describes Jesus' inquisition by the high priest, chief priests, elders and scribes (verse 53). Mark records how various witnesses for and against Jesus were called by the council, and the subsequent confusion, due to the contradictions within their statements (verse 59). It is Jesus' response to this that I find so impressive and so moving. To all the false testimony which would have provoked, in most people, angry reaction, Jesus we are told, "held his peace and answered them nothing."

I find that demonstration of inner strength and unwavering patience in the face of extreme provocation to be the example that shows that "love is not easily provoked."

It is interesting to note that the name of one particular disciple occurs in that passage. He was a distant observer and he was a man who is almost notorious for his readiness to be provoked! I refer, of course, to Peter who "followed him afar off, even unto the palace of the high priest" (verse 54); Peter who was "easily provoked" to protest when Jesus insisted on washing his feet (John 13:6); Peter who was "easily provoked" by Jesus' thrice repeated question: "Do you really love me?" (John 21:15–17 "lovest thou me?") and who showed his irritation by his anxiety to know what would happen to the favoured John, "the disciple whom Jesus loved" (John 21:20–22).

Perhaps it is by looking at these reactions to provocative situations that the clue to the nature of the love that is not easily provoked becomes clear.

Irritation, provocation, quickness to take offence is something that arises very often, not so much from conscious dislikes, as from feelings deep in the unconscious part of us. I spoke earlier of the reality and nature of "the unconscious", that part of us in which all our memories and experiences from the beginning of life are recorded.* In "filing them away" or dismissing them, especially unpleasant associations, into the unconscious (the process of "repression"), they do not cease to be active or potentially active. It needs some association — someone who reminds us of an unhappy relationship in the past for example — to "trigger" off these feelings. Peter's feelings about John, in that quotation above for example, were perhaps normally hidden or controlled, but they show themselves in his question. Peter's irritation with Jesus for his three-fold repetition of a question, the answer to which he would claim was never in doubt, was all the more tense just because such love for His Lord was *not* an assumption that he could sustain. He had failed earlier in his denial of Christ — three times, significantly — after defiant assurances that such a failure could not happen. It was indeed a "touchy" area for him.

Negative reaction to something, especially in situations in which we should react positively, is often expressed in irritation and in being "easily provoked." If someone criticises us — or a special friend — very immediate, though often quite irrelevant, reaction is stimulated. Indeed over-reaction is a very prevalent symptom of a lack of that inner peace, calm and security which our Lord so demonstrably had. It is only when deep inner peace and the tranquillity of serene cohesion has come into our souls and made them their dwelling-place, that we find we do not need to react superficially or negatively or irrationally to the provocative pressures of irritating situations. Jesus "answered nothing." He did not need to respond to the provocation for nothing that had been said really touched him at all.

Just there lies the difference between Peter and his Lord. Imagine the reaction of a man like Peter to such impertinence and such blasphemy. The man who unsheathed his sword in the Garden of Gethsemane would certainly have risen to the taunts of these soul-less inquisitors. But Jesus had an innate calm and dignity that expressed so much more effectively the way to deal with trivial nonsense.

There indeed we see the love that is not easily provoked. It was there in the Christ whose inner strength was the presence in him, at every level, of the very nature of love itself — for, as I keep stressing, God *is* Love. The more the Holy Spirit dwells in our innermost being, the less shall we be "easily provoked."

The God whose nature is love, is himself not easily provoked. He is "long-suffering." He is "patient." He does not easily reject. He does forgive. It is the glory of our faith that we believe in an accepting God whose desire is that we become whole, however long it may take. It is for our comfort to realise that even our constant failing to be all we should be, will not easily provoke him. His loving kindness is too deep and his tender mercy too wide to react in petty irritation to our perverse and foolish ways. The father who waits with dignity and in love for the prodigal son represents truly the divine patience rather than the easily provoked elder brother, irritated by the injustice of life.

It is all too easy to be as human as the elder brother. It is our task to reflect rather the love divine that is never "easily provoked."

Chapter 9

The Love that thinks no evil

The panorama of that "Love divine, all loves excelling" which is laid out in this inspired Hymn of Love is so familiar in the words of the *Authorised Version* that the phrases we say by heart tend to be accepted without question or analysis. The phrase "Love thinketh no evil" is one such statement. It is worth stopping and reflecting a little on just what Paul is saying through it.

The word "think" always has cognitive and cerebral connections, so the way in which the sentence is translated in the *Authorised Version* is not wholly helpful. I suspect that, in fact, it is depth of feeling rather than thinking in an intellectual sense that Paul is anxious to touch. This possibility seems to be supported by the various ways the verse is translated in other versions.

The *Jerusalem Bible* and the *Revised Standard Version* both use a "feeling" word here. It is, indeed, a very strong one — "resentful." Love is never resentful. The *New English Bible* and Dr. Barclay go further in their efforts to interpret the dangerous attitude — from a spiritual view of life — that is inherent in Paul's words. The *NEB* says: "Love keeps no score of wrongs", while William Barclay writes: "Love never nurses its wrath to keep it warm."

It is on this totally negative element in "thinking evil" that we must focus our attention, for the process *is* a wholly destructive one. To think evil dams up the whole movement within us working towards sanctification and prevents our growing up into the stature of the fulness of Christ (Ephesians 4:13), or, as the *NEB* renders that phrase, "mature manhood measured by nothing less than the fulness of Christ." Resentment is "cherishing bitter feelings" about someone or some situation. The most important word there is "cherishing." "Keeping a score" is the *NEB's* way of saying it.

"Nursing our wrath to keep it warm" is Dr. Barclay's attempt to catch that "holding" attitude, the refusal to let go, that the word "cherishes" conveys. It is the *holding on* to negative, destructive feelings that is the essence of the spiritual danger in "thinking evil."

As I write this I begin to feel that "thinking evil" in the sense of "holding onto", harbouring, cherishing hostile and bitter thoughts leads ultimately towards that strange and disturbing phrase that Jesus used about "blasphemy against the Holy Ghost" (Matthew 12:31). I have written in *Creative Silence* of this sin, but it may well be worth stating here, very briefly, the important things that must be remembered when we use that phrase.

All too often, in pastoral situations, we meet people devastated by the belief that they have committed that sin. As a result, they have to endure a life of pain and misery, fear and dread, which is out of all proportion to anything they have done! I do not want, for one moment, to equate "thinking evil" with the sin against the Holy Spirit. I am simply making the point that it is something of the holding and cherishing of evil thoughts that is the beginning of a process that could end in a *wholly* negative destructive attitude. And that is the essence of that sin. For that sin is not one act — so often people relate their belief that they have committed it to some specific event or occasion about which they have abnormal guilt. It is the product of an attitude of mind that loses, progressively, the ability to distinguish between good and evil. It was the deadly condition that Jesus saw around him, when religious people had reached the stage where they could not distinguish the good they saw in action from evil. They actually said Christ was possessed by Beelzebub (Mark 3:22–30). To so confuse good and evil is to be in a condition of spiritual darkness in which repentance is near impossible. There is little hope of anyone who is so spiritually blind as to call Christ the devil finding the capacity to repent. And if there is no repentance, how can there be forgiveness?

It is likely then, as I said in *Creative Silence,* that anyone who is worried about having committed the sin has, by definition, not done so! It is the blindness that prevents such anxiety that is the symptom of the sin. The essence of the sin against the Spirit is the total loss of the spiritual sensitivity it represents.

I have taken space to make this point here and to make it again because of the distress this particular problem creates and to pinpoint the danger in a habitual "thinking evil." Nothing diminishes love more than the cherishing of bitterness. It destroys relationships, stunts spiritual growth and, if continued and developed (cherished, that is, or kept warm), it can only lead us into spiritual conditions that bring dark nights and empty days.

The life, death and resurrection of Jesus is a demonstration in history of God's refusal to "think evil" of the world, in any way, even when it is a world that despises and rejects him. It is love alone that flows out from the Eternal Heart, the love that is the product of compassion, the declaration of kindness and the epitome of patience.

Chapter 10

The Love that rejoices in the truth

"Love is not glad when things go wrong for others." So James Moffat translated this part of I Corinthians 13 (verse 6). William Barclay puts it: "Love finds nothing to be glad about when someone goes wrong, but is glad when truth is glad." "Love does not gloat over other men's sins, but delights in the truth" is the *New English Bible* rendering. "Love takes no pleasure in other people's sins, but delights in the truth" says the *Jerusalem Bible*.

The first half of this statement on the nature of love is of failure — at a very practical level. We are really talking about gossip, getting facts right; about newspapers, about the media. It is, sadly, a fact that some of the traditionally highest circulating newspapers are those which concentrate their attention on the things that go wrong for others, for there are certain newspapers that have titillated their readership with reports of court cases that give special attention to sordid and unsavoury details of sexual peccadilloes, deviation and perversion or just simply the unwise but human errors people can make in matters of personal relationships. I do not want to recall particular examples in this connection for I would, by doing so, simply help to keep alive in the memory matters that ought to be forgotten — as well as forgiven — by society. Regrettably, millions read with some kind of pleasure — or as Paul says "rejoicing" — the faults, foibles and failings of others. If ever the words "there but for the grace of God, go I" ought to be recalled with humility, it is when the self-righteous read, with smug self-satisfaction, of the lapses of others. No one can be involved in pastoral work at depth and in confidence without seeing very clearly that human failure afflicts the saint as well as the sinner, the educated as well as the simple, the religious as well as the non-religious, the distinguished as well as the unknown, the cleric as well as the layman, the devout as well as the apathetic, the strong as well as the weak. "There is none righteous, no, not one." "All", (if they are honest) "have sinned and come short of the glory of God." The Kingdom of Heaven will be peopled, not by perfect saints who had no contact with evil, but by those with long lists of failures who nevertheless, knowing their need of grace, agonised over "the law in their members" and prayed for release.

It is the same with gossip. It would be marvellous if we could all "speak the truth in love" all the time, but the reality is otherwise. It is not easy for any of us to avoid the pleasures of gossip, however apparently innocent, and to be free from finding some enjoyment in others' unhappiness. No one will admit to this at the conscious level, but an honest self-examination of our inner processes and delights may well convince us how susceptible we are to such "rejoicing in iniquity." It would be dishonest if I did not say that I have found this sin to be prevalent as much in the church as in the world. What makes it worse in ecclesiastical circles is the sanctified pretence that no such feelings are ever present! They are!

What is this strange feature of us all (let those who can exclude themselves from the generalisation do so if they will) that responds in some way to "iniquity?"

When I reflect on these practical things, there keep coming into my mind the old-fashioned words "original sin." I have discussed this term in other places (briefly in *Creative Silence,* chapter 9) and do not embark on a discussion of it in depth here. It is a phrase that will be laughed to scorn by modern psychologists and probably most modern theologians. I do not myself plead for a return to the words "original sin" but I am aware of the reality of the concept which this phrase from the past tries to express. There is an inner pressure towards "the negative" in life inherent in unredeemed human nature and it will not be immediately destroyed (or, for that matter, destroyed this side of heaven) when the miracle of redemption has begun. "Sanctification" or "growing into

Christ" is a long, hard struggle against those negative pressures, the product of our life experience (our personal unconscious) and taking into consideration the cumulative effects of the history of humanity (the collective unconscious) especially on the psychically negative side (the shadow side in Jungian psychological language). It is — I can only offer personal testimony, though I find corroboration so dramatically stated in the Romans passage to which I constantly refer (Romans 7:19–21) — more natural to be self-centred than God-centred, to seek first the other things and give "the kingdom of God and his righteousness" second place; not to love God with heart and soul and mind and strength or our neighbour as ourselves. Only the sanctifying grace of God in Christ, through the Holy Spirit, can begin to change the balance that is naturally on the negative side of these equations. But life in the here and now *is* a continuing conflict between the evil that we would not and the good we would. Redeeming grace will triumph in the end, but not always in the here and now. It is part of not wholly sanctified human nature, sometimes, to rejoice in iniquity rather than in the truth.

Love is of God and God is love (as I have repeatedly reminded). Christ *is* the Truth (John 14:6). The Holy Spirit *is* Truth (I John 5:6). God never finds pleasure (if I may speak in such human terms) in what goes wrong for us or in us. Love's gladness lies only in our integrity and wholeness. The gift of the Holy Spirit is given in order that that integrity and inner unity may be attained. It is only when that Spirit probes and penetrates our inner being to bring about the fundamental change that will be expressed in new patterns of action and reaction that we shall find gladness in the truth and never in the misfortunes of others, or in their sins and failures. Then, and then only, will the disciple reflect the God who is truly love. While we remain human — as we do through life — we shall still fall short of the perfection which is God's. No Christian who is realistic about the way the pressures of sin and evil work will ever be naïve about release from temptation or simplistic about the subtleties of sin. Nevertheless the degree to which we rejoice less and less in others' failures and failings and the measure by which we increasingly long for their good, will testify to our growing up in Christ and will demonstrate the reality of our progressing sanctification and spiritual maturity.

"Who shall deliver me from the body of this death?" was Paul's question in his dereliction (Romans 7:24) before he himself gave the triumphant answer (7:25), which is our continuing justification of the Christian proclamation and the Christian mission: "I thank God, *through Jesus Christ,* our Lord."

Chapter 11

The Love that bears, believes, hopes, endures

The four words that make up this statement about love sub-divide themselves into two categories, positive and negative. Love "believes" all and love "hopes" all convey a positive element while the fact that love "bears" all and "endures" all suggests at first sight attitudes with some, so it feels, negative factors in them.

We talk about "bearing" burdens and "enduring" hardship and so give a feeling of "resolute acceptance", "stolid submission" or even "brave resignation" over such tribulation. As love is, of course, a wholly positive word and a totally creative concept, I cannot think that Paul meant us to see any part of it in a negative way. Moreover, if love is of God and God is love, it is all the more true that he must be talking of positive ideas. There is nothing negative in God.

It may not be unhelpful to look, at this point, at another passage in which Paul seems to be using negative rather than positive words and yet is, clearly, seeking to provide positive help. This is the occasion where he writes: "I have learned, in whatsoever state I am, therewith to be content" (Philippians 4:11). Again there is that negative sound: "Make the best of it." "Grin and bear it." "Soldier on." The more I read these words however, the more convinced I am that we have a very positive statement within them. For what Paul is saying is, in fact, very creative indeed. "In every situation in which I have been" he says in effect, giving a list of very dramatic events and experiences, "I have found a creative opportunity. I have, within the limitations of any given set of circumstances, however intolerable, found a way to use these circumstances constructively. So I accept these limits as reality, as the things which cannot be changed, and I try to find in them and through them, satisfaction, fulfilment and true contentment."

That takes us so far in the direction of seeing these words

constructively and positively, but let us go now to the *New English Bible,* for it has, in its translation, added another dimension to our understanding of this passage. Here is the profound rendering that version gives us: "I have learned to find resources in myself whatever the circumstances." Limitation, hostility and adversity are, spiritually, learning situations. They develop our inner resources, and so increase our faith at the same time evolving in us greater maturity.

It is, I am quite certain, in this positive sense that Paul uses "bearing" and "enduring." Love has an ability to take adverse circumstances and see in them opportunity for spiritual growth. "Man's extremity is God's opportunity" it has been said. Indeed it is. To bear and to endure, in terms of love, means taking and accepting, even grasping what is apparently to our hurt and redeeming it so that it becomes a spiritually beneficial experience. If adversity, disappointment and hostility can be accepted in this way, then the "bearing" and "enduring" are growth processes.

It is, of course, crucial for growing Christians that we should develop the capacity to learn from life in this way. It is also essential that we are able to help others to see suffering in this context too. It is essential, I would further argue, that we should see our own unacceptable side — the stranger within us — in this light and offer, as strangers need, hospitality. We must not only welcome that strange and threatening stranger within us, but see the new presence as the area of our greatest potential growth. To get to know that stranger and make "it" feel at home is to open the door to supreme opportunity for creative development. Only if we accept our weakness, failure, sin, potential for evil and degradation with open arms can we, in the end, embrace the opportunity the redemption of our unacceptable self makes possible.

Love divine is the love made manifest in Christ. There for ever emblazoned on the scenario of life is the only way to deal with evil. Calvary was not an event Christ bore with resignation or endured with bitterness. While the pain of facing all it involved compelled him to express, in prayer, the human wish that this cup might pass from him, his inner conviction about having to go to Jerusalem to suffer these things was always dominant within him. By accepting the whole awful process in the way he did, death turned into resurrection, and apparent defeat was transformed into victory. Golgotha became the Garden of Resurrection.

It is this principle from the very heart of the Gospel that Paul reflects in his understanding of his own imprisonment, beatings, tribulations, persecutions, violence, etc. Life for him, because of his being called to discipleship, could not be without the suffering endemic to that call. It could however become creative opportunity and therefore true contentment if the inner resources were there.

Love bears . . .

Let us turn now to the first of these four words in more detail. There is some evidence for a textual variation in the word translated "bear", for Cyprian at least knew a variant reading meaning "cherishes" (*stergei* for *stegei*). That is an attractive possibility, for the word "cherish" is a beautiful one. It means, by derivation, "holding dear." To follow this interpretation might, however, be the heart taking over from the head, without much to justify the move! I must therefore keep to the word "bears," but stress the point I have been making above. "Bears" must not be taken simply as "quiet, brave endurance" (to quote somewhat surprisingly from a wedding hymn*) but must be seen as a positive, creative word. *Per ardua ad astra:* it is through hardship that we reach the stars. It is "through dying we live" (II Corinthians 6:9). All we have to "bear" in life is a gateway to growth, if we can but use the experiences we have as media of learning.

The translations add various strands to the concept of bearing all things. The *New English Bible* puts it thus: "There is nothing love cannot face", an example of "accentuating the positive" (as a popular song of yesteryear said) by duplicating the negative! The *Jerusalem Bible* chooses the phrase: "Love is always ready to excuse." William Barclay translates thus:

O perfect Love (Dorothy Frances Gurney)

"Love can stand any kind of treatment." What does it mean then to say of divine love "Love bears all things?"

The elements are among those we have already noted in our journey into and through love as Paul proclaims it. There is the divine patience with which the long-suffering God waits and waits and waits for the prodigal, drawn by the "cords of love", to return. There is the divine kindness which, desiring our good, will never stampede us into the kingdom of God, but respecting our personalities, will lead us gently to the living water. The process may involve bearing many things, standing many kinds of treatment, suffering rejection and personal crucifixion, but divine love bears it all "enduring the cross, despising the shame" (Hebrews 12:2). There is the divine forgiveness, forgiving "till seventy-times seven" (Matthew 18:22), infinite in mercy, "bearing all things" to bring back one soul.

It is on the capacity of divine love to bear all things in order to win the heart of human beings that the attitude of human love wholly rests. The demand it creates is frightening for it asks of us so much that we cannot, in our frailty, give; but the demand remains. We must then endeavour, with grace, to bear the unbearable, endure the unendurable, be patient with those who try our patience, be kind to those who make themselves intolerable, be loving to those whom we find it hard to love, "forbearing one another in love" (Ephesians 4:2) always, for Christ's sake.

This is not a demand of a romantic or an idealistic kind. It is not a plea for a patience that is weakness, a kindness that is soft, a sympathy that is sentimental or a forgiveness that is meek and mild. The divine love incarnate was seen in a man of courage, physical and spiritual, who, in the hour of his ultimate suffering, could cry: "Father, forgive them for they know not what they do" (Luke 23:34). This surely is to "bear all things", to "stand any kind of treatment." There was "nothing love did not face."

We cannot, in our human weakness, emulate such a love divine for it is beyond all human love in attainment, but we

are never free to stop trying to reflect the love that bore all
things and bears them still.

Love believes . . .

"Love believes all things, hopes all things." While we deal
with the word "believes", we keep an eye on the truly positive
word "hopes." For with belief and hope united we are in the
realms of *faith* and *trust* and *promise.* To say anything about
our "beliefs" is to touch on a very fundamental part of us, for
our belief determines everything we do. Without belief we can
do nothing. With belief, we have a promise which makes all
things possible.

This aspect of faith and trust is reflected in the way "Love
believeth all things" is rendered in some of the other versions.
"Love is ready to trust" says the *Jerusalem Bible.* William
Barclay puts it, in a very dramatic sentence: "Love's first
instinct is to believe in people." First instinct? The reference is
indeed to very primary attitudes.

As has been the case in every part of this series of
reflections, I apply the phrase first to the divine love and ask
just what is it that we are saying. Let us look more closely at
William Barclay's translation.

It is the "first instinct" of God, in his love, to believe in
people. Of course this vibrates as true in the deep places of
the soul. The whole of God's redemptive activity is based on
the assumption that, no matter what happens, no matter how
catastrophically man, in his freedom behaves, it is still true
that, in the end (for "love suffers long"), the prodigal will
"come to himself" and make for home. So here, as we have
seen, is the meaning of "kind." Love seeks our good without
ever denying our personalities. And love is prepared to wait
and wait and wait, at great cost, to show that it "believes in
people", sticking to that belief whatever happens.

The divine love can do this only if there is in God a real
sense of hope. The union of love and hope in this chapter is
no accident. They always belong together. There is a divine
optimism at the heart of the universe that sees the end of

everything as redemption, renewal, integration, wholeness and unity. This is the direction of the divine activity *all* the time and love will never lose that "first instinct" to believe in people made in the image of God.

The obligation for the disciple to have a similar belief in people is inescapably transferred. But how difficult it is to practise! People do disappoint us, let us down, deny us and betray us. These are facts of life, as they relate to our personal lives. Disappointment and indeed betrayal are also part of the life corporate. We live in what seems sometimes to be an era of increasing gracelessness. It is often hard to have "optimistic joy" (Romans 12:12 *WB*), to keep believing in people. The world we live in seems dominated by violence, indiscipline, commercialism and sensualism. It is a world in which courtesy, grace and things of "good report" have too little place. Yet we must keep history in perspective. It has all happened before — as Romans, chapter 1 makes clear. However the *scale* on which gracelessness now seems to exist and the fact that it is "global" in context, strains our ability to retain that "first instinct" about people. Not least is it difficult in the realm of politics, national and international.

In our human weakness this contemporary despair may be authentic, but it must not take us over. On the cross itself, Christ reached the point of just such despair, yet found the strength to say: "Father, forgive them for they know not what they do" (Luke 23:34). The concentration of wickedness that produced the cross was part of the human capacity for evil, demonstrated in such ghastly ways in the course of history. But not even all that humans at their horrific worst could do, nullified the possibility of Christ being raised again to heal and to make whole. For the empty Cross, like the empty grave, speaks of faith and hope and a belief in the ultimate redemption of everything, the final triumph of good over evil.

It is not the way of divine love to give humanity up. The divine love holds to its primary instinct which is to believe in people, and it acts on that principle. We therefore have no choice in the matter. If our love is to follow the pattern of the divine love, we must work and pray on the premise that there is the possibility of good in every man and woman, in every situation. Love does "believe all things." It must be "ready to trust." It must recognise that there is "no limit to its faith" in people. This is not an invitation to fantasy. Nor is it false piety. It is the way in which God acts, and so it must be the way for the disciples, too.

Love hopes . . .

"Three things last for ever — faith, hope, love" Paul writes (in William Barclay's translation). He then goes on to select as "the greatest of these" love. With that judgement, none will disagree. The fact that love is the greatest of them all does not, however, diminish "faith" and "hope." It is then a matter for gladness that in this great Hymn of Love, there is a phrase that compels us to consider the great quality of hope. Love "hopeth all things."

To see "hope" in its true perspective, I return to the image of the "map" that is the Christian's overall view of life. For many, possibly even for most (and I say this not judgementally, but only as a statement of what seems to be fact), the map of life in terms of which all important assessments are made as valid and relevant is strictly bounded by limits that arise from a "this world" view of everything. That which is real is temporal. Anything outside these boundaries, if it exists at all, is at most a possible extra to life, but is not the focal point of life or even of serious importance to it.

This is a totally inadequate view of life as the Christian sees it. It is of the essence of Christian faith to hold that "the things that are seen are temporal." It is "the things that are not seen that are eternal." There are, it is clear and as I have already said, two quite different ways of looking at "reality" and the result of our choice of these ways determines everything we do and are. Our aims in life depend on which view we take. The perspective we have determines our values.

Hope is related to the map which takes in the eternal

dimension as the primary fact of life. It is a true optimism based on the reality of forces, energies and powers, that belong to that divine dimension. If our map only takes in this world and all that goes on in it, there is comparatively little ground for hope. Hope comes when faith projects that dimension of the spiritual into our perspective on life and makes it not an extra element, but the essential one.

This is borne out by the relationship that hope has, in the New Testament, to life after death (for example I Corinthians 15:19). Hope is based on the reality of the risen Christ, as the Christian Church experienced him. If there is no risen Christ, no resurrection, Paul tells us, we are the most miserable of people! We have no *hope*. The Church is the company of people who can truly hope. They have the proper perspective on life, on its events and on its history. It is a perspective given through the risen and living Christ, still present and active in the power of the Holy Spirit. In the deepest possible sense, they can feel that, in the long run, the divine dimension provides that all will be truly well. That is Christian hope.

In writing of the love that bears all things and believes all things, I have constantly stressed that principle which is fundamental to my exposition of the Hymn of Love. What I am describing all the time is the nature of the *Divine* attitude to his people. Just as the infinite loving-kindness and tender mercy leads one to the divine patience and the divine kindness, so it is true to say that it is of the very nature of God to bear all that man, in his hardness of heart, will produce and to believe in his people. Equally love hopes all things too. Once again it is William Barclay who brings out the full meaning of that hope in his magnificent version: "Love never regards anyone or anything as hopeless."

That, for me, sums it up. For the Christian nothing is hopeless and no one is beyond hope. That is God's attitude to events as he points us towards a view that takes spiritual facts, factors and forces into the evolution of our lives. This is God's attitude to people as he descends into hell to recover and redeem. It has been said that there is a road that leads to hell even from the very gate of heaven. That may be, but it is much more comforting to know that there is a road to heaven from the very gates of hell. Love *never* regards anyone as beyond hope.

The disciple must build his or her attitude on hope too. It is of the essence of Christian belief not to set limits to faith so the Christian must have a fundamentally hopeful attitude to life and people. This does not mean easy optimism or superficial judgement, nor does it equal pious imagination. Hope is *always* realistic. It has no illusions about the things that can go wrong and do go wrong in life. What it does do is base its attitudes on ultimate realities. In doing that we "live by hope."

We are saved by hope, we read (Romans 8:24). Hope is indeed our salvation for it lifts our eyes from the immediate and the material to a perspective divinely conditioned. From that perspective, love "never faileth", "love hopeth all things." Neither love divine, nor its human reflection, however frail, can ever regard anyone or anything as hopeless.

Love endures . . .

Once again it is to William Barclay that I turn for illumination, through his translation in verse 7, of the phrase: "Love endureth all things." While the other versions confine themselves to variations of the form we have in the *Authorised Version* (as for example in the *New English Bible* phrase: "there is no limit to love's endurance", or the *Jerusalem Bible:* "Love endures what comes"), Dr. Barclay somehow gives the words another dimension when he writes: "Nothing can happen that can break love's spirit." I like that way of saying that love endures all things, immensely.

If the nature of the divine love is expressed in this phrase, the door is open to a sense of security and assurance. If God is one who, no matter what happens, extends his arms in love and welcome — as the parable of the prodigal son suggests — then so much of the sense of guilt that pastors meet, is totally unnecessary. The divine forgiveness is real. The divine ability to accept is beyond our understanding because it goes so much further than human attitudes in the face of wrong, evil and attack. So often people refuse to *feel* forgiven, when it is certain that forgiveness has been given. Yet acceptance of the intellectual proposition "God forgives" is not the same as *knowing that statement to be true for oneself* in very specific situations. Because the refusal to *feel* forgiven remains a factor in the personality, the possibility that overwhelming guilt will express itself not only in sadness, anxiety, desperation or suicide, but even in psychosomatic illness, becomes very present. Guilt, gnawing away at a troubled soul's inner being, may even express itself in forms of dis-ease that literally gnaw away the body.

It is indeed part of healing ministry to find a way to heal the memories of mistakes and mismanagement of long ago and even to ease the pressing and continuous guilt of present situations unconfessed or unresolved, where conflict between personal feelings and intuitions as to how Christians may behave conflicts with public or ecclesiastical definitions of morals. Guilt has been seen, in so many specific situations of unresolved conflict and tension within, to have created anxiety to the point of illness and death, both symbolically and literally.

This is an area in which we have to learn and to express the principle of love expounded in this book. The preacher, the teacher, the pastor, the "carer", must always be sensitive to unresolved guilt in those to whom each ministers. So many lives of great potential have been nearly destroyed when those who are down and out emotionally, mentally, physically and spiritually because of failure of one kind or another, have met and had to face the condemnation of fellow-Christians and the judgement of the church, when they expected understanding and love.

It is not possible to give illustrations of this sort of situation for all the examples would be drawn from real life. To do this even in generalised ways would not necessarily prevent the possible identification of people who suffered from such guilt feelings, whether or not there was any reality in the link, nor would it encourage confidence in that essential of all pastoral care and concern, confidentiality. Everyone involved in such ministry is absolutely bound by that principle. There is nothing worse than a pastor who cannot help discussing his parishioners' problems publicly or semi-publicly. Nevertheless the points I am making are all rooted in real-life situations. What I seek to do is to bring the comfort of the Christian gospel, in general terms, to those who may fall, unhappily, in these categories and hope that the assurance and security in this phrase — "Love endureth all things" — can bring them strength. There will be "balm in Gilead" for them. There is nothing that breaks love's spirit, if there is genuine repentance. Forgiveness is available if it will be accepted.

There are two comments that arise in this context. The first relates to a matter with which I have already dealt — the sin against the Holy Spirit. I mention it again briefly here for it seems to be the import of Jesus' statement that this is the one thing that could do just that. I simply repeat the main point. It was not the wrong things the Pharisees did that constituted that awful sin. It was the spiritual blindness they demonstrated that was evidence of an inability to see their condition. In other words, there was almost no possibility of repentance because they were so unaware of their state. That was dangerous indeed, for it did involve the risk of the ultimate sin. Guilt, by definition, is a statement of anxiety that arises from the knowledge that we have sinned. The very presence of a sense of guilt states categorically that it cannot be the condition Jesus described.

Secondly the statement that nothing can happen that will break love's spirit is not a charter for licence. There is, as Paul had to tell the Corinthians, an essential difference between liberty and licence. We are not free to do as we like because God's grace is real. We are not free to sin "that grace may abound." This is a travesty of Christianity and its understanding of the Christian life. The Christian cannot do what he likes because "it is going to be all right in the end anyway." What we do know is that nothing can happen that will change the divine attitude to human beings, nor is there anything that we can ourselves do that is serious enough to damage the fundamental basis on which the divine-human relationship stands. The initiative within that relationship is from God and it is an initiative of love. The response sought from human beings is one of love too ... "we love him because he first loved us" (I John 4:19). Within that relationship of mutual love, divinely based, nothing can happen that can break love's spirit.

It is supremely important that preaching should, whatever else it does, offer the word of comfort (and "comfort" by derivation, is connected with strengthening) to the soul in despair. "I came not to condemn but to save", our Lord said in drawing attention to the purpose of his coming (John 3:17). That statement is specific and absolutely fundamental for our understanding of the Gospel. The Gospel is not a gospel of dis-couragement and should never be made that. It is foreign to the purpose of God in the Incarnation. It is a Gospel of en-couragement and no pastor or teacher, preacher or priest dare ever forget that primary fact. There is no situation so low, no crisis so appalling, no guilt so overwhelming that it can "break love's spirit" if there is true repentance in the troubled heart. Christ descended into hell (as our creeds put it) to reach and touch the lowest depths of evil, because he was at that very time on his way to the Garden of the Resurrection.

If this be the way of God — and I have consistently, if repeatedly, said it is, then it is the way of the disciple to be "as his Master." How, in the realities of life, each of us has to work this out, is something we all have to face. What is clear is that the spirit of love within us can, through the increase of faith, hope and love, enable us to face all that comes, with quiet calm and inner peace. Moreover as we, each one, can understand our own security within the divine-human relationship, knowing that nothing can break it from God's side, so we can create in others something of that same sense of security through our own spirit of love towards them, a spirit that will not be broken by disappointment, resentment, betrayal or anything else.

Ours is a high calling and none of us will reach perfection in it. But that we are called to endeavour, with the help of the Holy Spirit, to reach that standard can never be questioned.

Chapter 12

The Love that lasts for ever

Loved with everlasting love,
Led by grace that love to know . . .

So wrote George Wade Robinson in the well-known hymn.

It is the word "everlasting" on which I want to concentrate as we turn to the tremendous words in verse 8 of this great Hymn of Love — "love never faileth." Reaching this phrase is rather like breaking through the clouds as the plane ascends and emerges into the infinite sunshine always above them. We climb into a stratum of knowledge that is not cognitively acquired. It is received through intuition. Though that knowledge is expressed in lyrical terms, it still deals with reality; the reality of "the things that are eternal." "Love never faileth." In human weakness it does — over and over again. But the divine love is the love that does not fail — ever.

The word "ever" takes us back to this key concept of "everlasting." In the context of his perspective of the "ages", Paul sees love as that which goes on far beyond the present age, an age which will pass away. That "end of the present age" was seen by Paul, as it was seen by the early church as a whole, as imminent. Christians lived then as if the world they knew would soon come to an end and the "new age" begin.

In such circumstances, all that belongs to the present — even including prophecy and tongues, will pass away but "love does not come to an end" (*New English Bible*). "Love lasts for ever" (William Barclay). It is in that sense of "everlasting" that "love never faileth." It is this that "abides." That which is only "in part" shall be "done away", "when that which is perfect is come." Love is there, constant, unchangeable. When we see, not "through a glass darkly" but

"face to face", love remains. Love *is* "everlasting love."
"Love lasts for ever."

I have referred repeatedly to this passage as a *Hymn* of
Love. By doing this, I am underlining the lyrical nature of the
whole passage. The fullness of the divine love is expressed
poetically. Indeed, Paul's ability to rise to extraordinary
heights of true insight and knowledge is expressed here in as
sublime a way as he ever attains. If the hymn be wholly his —
and I am not aware of any serious critical doubts on this
point — it is one of the most dramatically moving passages in
the Bible. It is superbly constructed and spiritually so sublime
and profound. There is no doubt that such a statement could
only come through a mind and a soul with (Ephesians 3:17
NEB) "deep roots and firm foundations." It could only be
written "in the Spirit." But is such poetic vision and
enlightened awareness so lyrical that it feels totally unrelated
to the real lives we all have to live?

One of Paul Tillich's books is entitled *On the Boundary*. It
is, like others he has written, autobiographical in a reflective
kind of way. It is a statement of his experience of the stance
he found himself forced to take in his life. He lives "on the
frontier" — between, for example, city and country, reality
and imagination, theology and philosphy, native land and
alien land, church and society, religion and culture, idealism
and Marxism, etc. The Christian has to take up his position in
relation to life, on the same basis. Here (that is in this world)
he has "no permanent home" (Hebrews 13:14 *NEB*) but he
seeks "one to come." He is, in terms of Jesus' profound
prayer for his disciples (John 17:15–16), to be "in" the world,
but not "of" it. He lives "on the boundary" between them.
The disciple has to relate realistically to seen but temporal
things, but he knows intuitively that it is the "not seen" (II
Corinthians 4:18) things that are eternal and ultimately true
reality. He is on the frontier between the physical and the
spiritual yet must be related actively to both. He cannot help
but feel the tensions that arise — for example in ethical
questions — as the two realms impinge on each other. If he

slips off the boundary to one side or to the other, he loses the essential balance that is so important for creative Christian living. To reduce "the physical" until it plays no proper part in living is to deny the Incarnation and to diminish the value of life in the here and now. To fail to give "the spiritual" a proper place is to lose the vital factor in determining the proper balance of the Christian life, for the spiritual dimension always has a "priority among equals." Jesus was truly human and truly divine and no view of Christ makes sense if either statement is weakened, but similarly in that priority among equals, the divine takes first place for he was the eternal Christ ("before Abraham was, I am", John 8:58) and he returned through resurrection and ascension to be with God the Father. The Christian's base in the "eternal dimension" demands a real and total involvement in the world in which Jesus was tempted "like as we are" and even suffered in a way none of us has had to suffer. He was "in" the world indeed. Yet he could not and would not be "of" the world.

It is the reality of the Incarnation of the Christ "born of the Virgin Mary, crucified under Pontius Pilate" that ensures that Paul's Hymn of Love is not pure fantasy, but is the sound and solid base on which all Christian life is founded. We are called to love God and our neighbour in this world just because we belong, in spiritual terms, to that other eternal world.

The nature, quality, depth and sacrifice to which we are called is grounded in the divine love which "never faileth." Though heaven and earth pass away, the love which is of God "lasts for ever." We cannot, knowing our persistent human weakness and failure, begin to pretend that our human love has the divine "everlasting" quality about it that it should have. Fail we shall, repeatedly and miserably. But the standard is set. Our constant desire and prayer must be for the gift of more of that unfailing love to be within us, for it is unfailing love we are to offer to the world in his name.

Chapter 13

Listen to Love

Verses 8–12 are about knowledge, the full knowledge that will come when the whole picture, in the divine perspective, is seen. There are two kinds of knowledge — as we have already noted. There is the knowledge that is "partial" and there is the knowledge that will be "whole." "My knowledge now is partial; then it will be whole like God's knowledge of me" (verse 12, *NEB*). I would like to look a little more closely at the two kinds of knowledge of which Paul is aware.

For help with this I turn to another of his letters, that to the Ephesians. One of the reasons church people want to adhere to the *Authorised Version* is the sheer beauty of its language. While the *New English Bible* has given us rich clarification, it has seldom equalled the great, high levels of poetic expression or the dignity of prose for so long associated with the King James Bible. There is, however, one passage that may have reached equality with the *Authorised Version* and perhaps even surpassed it, in terms of beauty of language and a sublime use of words. It is the section to which I now turn — Ephesians 3:14–21.

As the passage may not be familiar to everyone, I set it out in full. It is the extraordinary statement which Paul makes on knowledge to which I seek to draw attention. He writes to the Ephesians thus:

"With this in mind, then, I kneel in prayer to the Father, from whom every family in heaven and on earth takes its name, that out of the treasures of his glory he may grant you strength and power through his Spirit in your inner being, that through faith Christ may dwell in your hearts in love."

"With deep roots and firm foundations, may you be strong to grasp, with all God's people, what is the breadth and length and height and depth of the love of Christ, and to know it, though it is beyond knowledge. So may you attain to fullness of being, the fullness of God himself."

"Now to him who is able to do immeasurably more than all we can ask or conceive, by the power which is at work among us, to him be glory in the church and in Christ Jesus from generation to generation evermore!"

This passage is all about faith and love and in many ways links with I Corinthians 13. It is however to that amazing statement about knowledge that I draw your attention. "To *know* (the love of Christ) *though it is beyond knowledge.*" This is paradox indeed . . . an encouragement to "know" what is not able to be known!

There is only one possible conclusion. Paul is talking about two kinds of knowledge. There is a knowledge of a rational, intellectual, cognitive kind and there is a knowledge which we attain in a totally different way. That way must be an intuitive way, a way related to attributes like feeling, imagination and sensitivity, a way that can only be possible through the antennae of the soul.

Within the Hymn of Love, this distinction in knowledge is recognised. Though I have the gift of all knowledge Paul writes, it is, without love, "as nothing." There is a possibility of reaching the heights of cognitive knowledge in this earthly life, but that sort of knowledge is not the kind of knowledge of which Paul seems to speak in verse 12. We are here in the realm of the knowledge that is peculiar to the soul. It is not the product of a rational process. This kind of knowledge we can certainly have in this life, but it can only be "in part", "partial." Only in the life of eternity can that knowledge be complete, for in that life we shall know and be known. This indeed is knowledge in that second and deeper sense.

The love that (verse 8, *WB*) "lasts for ever", the love that is "divine, all loves excelling", the love that is "of God" is a love that is intimately associated with the knowledge available to the soul, so much so that the knowledge is impossible without love.

It is that "knowledge of the soul" that is so important in determining how much of the divine love we can reflect. It is a knowledge that comes through Christ and in the initiating action of the Holy Spirit. It is the knowledge available to those who long for living relationship with divine love, the love of God the Father. It is from such inner knowledge that the capacity to reflect the divine love in life comes for it is out of our deep understanding in a relationship with him that the sources and springs of the patience, kindness and forgiveness that are of God are "rooted and grounded." We cannot be in touch with the "fullness of God himself" (which can only be attained through knowledge of the length, breadth, depth and height of the love of Christ) unless with "deep roots and firm foundations" we have been "strong to grasp" that divine love. Then of course, in terms of our "eternal triangle of love", it goes out into the community in Christ's name.

So the Hymn of Love is not just a lyrical song about love. It is a statement of the very bases on which we build our lives, personal and corporate, in the ministry of love.

We love because we "know." The more we "know", the more we love.

Listen to love, for such listening leads to the heart of the Gospel.

Chapter 14

Put Love first

The phrase "first among equals" (*primus inter pares*) is not unknown in church circles. It is certainly familiar in presbyterian polity where it describes the essential parity of its clergy with a recognition that one is deliberately chosen to preside, as moderator, over its affairs for a limited period but in no way does it destroy the equality of the ministry in that system. Love is, in a sense, similarly first among equals. Faith, hope and love all "last for ever" (*NEB, WB*), "abide" (*AV*), but the greatest of them must be love.

It is from *outside* the thirteenth chapter that we take the phrase I have used from time to time, "the best way of all", for it is the *New English Bible* version of the AV's "more excellent way" (chapter 12, verse 31). Similarly the phrase with which I seek to round off this part of our reflections on *Love, the Word that heals,* also falls outside the traditional break marked by the end of a chapter. "Follow after love" is the first statement in chapter 14, or, as the *New English Bible* says, very simply: "Put love first." This is the natural consequence to the presentation of love which we have been given. "Spare no effort to possess love" says William Barclay in his translation. "You must want love more than anything else" the *Jerusalem Bible* tells us.

So, wondrously, the gift of love is given. It is the greatest gift of all to receive and to give. But the reality of the gift does not mean we do not have to struggle and strive to reach the high standards we seek and which God asks. So it is right that we should be told to "spare no effort to possess love." There is always effort involved in spiritual achievement. "You must want love more than anything else" and accept the pain and discipline demanded. I do not mean love has to be earned. It does not, for it is wholly a gift. But the struggle to reflect it is always there. "How can I love ...?" the cry will come spontaneously. How can I love those whom I dislike? those who drive me to despair and desperation? those who set out to destroy me? those who represent everything I dislike? The command remains — love must be put first.

Constantly I have reminded that all our human love must take, as a pattern, the divine love. That is a love which accepted a betrayal for thirty pieces of silver, denial three times by his right-hand man and the insensitive cruelty of crucifixion by people who "knew not what they did." To reach such heights of love was a gift from God, but that does not cancel out as irrelevant the strength required to accept and forgive such denial or the ability to cope with such insufferable torture as crucifixion. No wonder that "being in agony, he prayed more earnestly", evidence if ever any were needed of the struggle taking place in his soul, and of the effort *he* had to make.

The way of love will always be spiritually profitable but never easy. There may even be darkness and at times desperation on the loving pilgrim's path, as the endless struggle between "flesh" and "spirit" goes on. But all who seek the way of love that Paul depicts will be encouraged.

To walk the way of love demands faith. To keep on walking along that way, whatever happens, demands hope. So faith and hope are essential components in the process which leads to life abundant.

The best way of all.

Spare no effort to possess love.

It is the Word that heals.

PART II

THE HEALING WORD

Chapter 15

The Healing Word

"Love is the Word that heals." That has been the theme of our journey through love so far. The divine love is a healing love. The love we can offer that follows the divine pattern is healing love too. I want now to apply our title very specifically to the Word who was made flesh and dwelt among us as the great first chapter of John's Gospel tells us. God is Love. Jesus is the Love of God incarnate, the Word made flesh. This is the source of all our healing. It is the Word, Jesus Christ, God incarnate, that is the Healing Word. He brings divine love. He is divine love. Love is the Word that heals indeed.

Here we are drawn inevitably to the great *Logos* passage that introduces John's Gospel. The unfamiliarity of the word *Logos* to many people — and the limitations of the word *"Word"* in English — have made this important passage of scripture a problem to many — and to the translators! J. B. Phillips, for example, in his *New Testament in Modern English* offers the paraphrase:

"At the beginning, God expressed himself. That personal expression, that word was with God and was God, and he existed with God from the beginning."

The Healing Word is Christ himself. But John's use of this concept is special to him in the New Testament (I say "special" not "unique", for in Paul and in the Letter to the Hebrews there are allusions to the kind of ideas John is expressing so profoundly) and so we must examine the ideas he is trying to use and the teaching he seeks to convey through this particular description of the cosmic Christ.

Logos, classically, means "reason." The New Testament use of it related much more to the (classical also) meaning "word." Taken by John however, and used in the way he uses it, *Logos* takes on a profoundly religious, theological and spiritual content, almost indefinable, but absolutely real and authentic. The *Logos* now becomes the declaration of *the divine Word* and so of the divine will. It is both Christ the Word and the Word of God. The whole is "the divine plan of salvation" and in this, of course, it is gloriously expressing the purpose of Christ in his Incarnation. So the *Word*, the *Logos* was made flesh — for our salvation — and "dwelt among us."

This is a wonderful way of expressing the truth of the Gospel in another form. In so doing, it introduces a dimension of enormous depth into the Gospels' combined witness to the "Immanuel" — "God with us" — Christ. The living Christ of the roads of Palestine was the Healing Word in action. The living Christ of faith is the Healing Word today.

The concept of the *Logos* or *Word* is used by John to proclaim two great purposes. The first is that Christ is the *Revealer of God* and the second that he is the *Saviour of man*. In both capacities, he is the Healing Word.

If the incarnate Christ reacts to hypocrisy as he did when he met it in the accusing Pharisees, "tempting" Sadducees or supercilious scribes, then we are seeing the way in which God looks at hypocrisy and deals with it. So wherever hypocrisy is offered as a way of life, the judgement of God must be on it. That is made clear in the way in which the Word/Logos made flesh dealt with it in his sojourn on earth.

If the incarnate Christ can look with much more understanding and sympathy on a woman taken in adultery than on her accusers, then we know how God sees the relationship between the erring good and the unholy righteous. Jesus' attitude in that — and other stories — reveals the nature and will of God as it is and not as ecclesiastics have so often proclaimed it to be.

As the incarnate Christ endures suffering and temptation, pain and death, so the divine empathy with those who suffer all these things is shown to be beyond question. It is this, the revelation of the nature of God, that comes through the *Logos,* the Word, the Healing Word.

That healing purpose at the heart of God would remain the expression of an idea were it not for its demonstration in the sequence of acts of grace that make up the Christian Gospel. "The divine plan of Salvation" is, as we now see it, the Incarnation, Crucifixion and Resurrection of Christ, followed by the promised gift of the Holy Spirit.

All this is involved in the concept of the eternal *Logos,* the eternal Word, who was with God in the beginning, is now and ever shall be, who lived as the historical Jesus and who rose again to (using the language of the Gospel story) "ascend to the right hand of God." The pre-existent Christ is Jesus of Nazareth, "my Beloved Son", crucified and risen. The whole plan and purpose of salvation is to restore humanity to that wholeness that is so desperately sought — oneness with God, through Christ, in the Spirit. Our integration is, indeed, through the Spirit of Christ, our Lord. The Logos is the Healing Word in that he reveals the healing heart of God and offers himself to provide the way that leads to life.

There are three statements it is helpful to make on The Healing Word.

First, the *Logos,* the *Word,* is not only concerned with speech but with *power.* We can listen to all that the Word, Jesus, had to *say* to us and be greatly blessed thereby — as the world has been for near 2,000 years. What is much more important is the realisation that He came to *be with us* (Immanuel means "God with us") and to *do things for us* that we could not do for ourselves. So the great plan of salvation, revealed by the Healing Word, Jesus Christ, is the demonstration in power, in history, of the mighty *acts* of God in Christ; "The Word was with God at the beginning and through him all things came to be." The Word is the power in creation and in the re-creation that is the redemption of mankind. There was life in him and that life was the light of men.

Secondly, I draw from Dr. Barclay's writing on St John's

Gospel this important point. "Both Jew and Greek possessed the conception of the *Logos* of God." So Christ did indeed come in the fullness of the time, at the right time, to be the medium of salvation and healing (they are words with common elements). So, not only for the individual, but for the world, Jesus, the *Logos,* is the Healing Word. He is relevant to and ready to be welcomed by men and women of every nation, culture, vocabulary or intellectual background, for in him is the power to transform, redeem, create, universally.

The third comment I take from Henry Drummond, the author of the great classic I have already mentioned, *The Greatest Thing in the World.* In response to criticism of his orthodoxy and integrity after he had published *Natural Law in the Spiritual World* and particularly *The Ascent of Man,* he re-affirmed to the great evangelist, Sankey, "my words . . . my deepest convictions." They are a tremendous acclamation of the Healing Word.

> "The power to set the heart right, to renew the springs of affection, comes from Christ. The sense of the infinite worth of a single soul, and the recoverableness of man at his worst are the gifts of Christ. The freedom from guilt, the forgiveness of sins, come from Christ's cross; the hope of immortality springs from Christ's grave . . ."

Christ is indeed the *Logos,* the Healing Word.

Chapter 16

Looking to Jesus

I want now to keep "looking unto Jesus" who is "the author and finisher of our Faith" (Hebrews 12:2) for he is, as we have seen, the Healing Word himself, *Logos,* Word made flesh, incarnate Son of God, Jesus the Christ. As that writer to the Hebrews put it in the Barclay version of verse 2: "All the time we must concentrate on nothing but Jesus, in whom our faith had its beginning and must have its end."

We are going now to "concentrate" on attributes and attitudes of this Healing Word, for what we find in this Word, Jesus, is the truth about God. The attributes we see in the Son are the attributes of the Father. The Son's attitudes reflect the divine nature itself.

It is an attribute of the Word that heals, whom we see as "love incarnate, love divine", that he *understands* the problems and pain of human beings. That is stated very simply and directly in John 2:24–25: "He knew what was in man . . . because he knew all men." Or, in Dr Barclay's version: "He did not need anyone to tell him about human nature because he was well aware what it is like."

The feeling of disillusionment over our failure to reach standards of life and love that reflect Christ is a feeling we all know. If people knew what we were really like; if the awful ghastly truth about us — our faults, our secret sins, our secret thoughts and desires known — how appalled they would be. Why, even Paul in reflection saw himself as the "chief of sinners" (I Timothy 1:15) and hated that he was just this.

The experience is an authentic one. It is, however, a sign that we are "on the move" spiritually, for it is a feeling only possible in those who sense what true goodness and the truly spiritual are like. The cry of confession and the longing for forgiveness "full and free" are signs of progress towards the life of the Spirit. They speak of growth in grace and the re-creation that is at work inwardly. That soul, now troubled, will , in God's own time, bear fruit.

I make this point about response to anticipated disillusionment because I feel that it reflects the kind of response that comes from the heart of God. "My thoughts are not your thoughts, neither are your ways, my ways" saith the Lord. The perspective from which God sees things and the way he "reads" a life are totally different from the limited interpretations that arise from a human perspective. That is why there is often an element of "divine surprise" when God's "view" is known — as Simon, the Pharisee found, in relation to the "woman of bad reputation" who washed our Lord's feet with her tears (Luke 7:36–50): as those who would stone the "woman taken in adultery" found as they shrank ignominiously away from their discomfiture.

This point must be taken seriously by all who seek to offer divine judgement on the sins of others. The mores of a time or a culture seldom coincide with the values of the Kingdom of God. Those who insist that they do might be dumb-founded if they had the ability to know the divine view of apparently "wrong" situations. It is so easy to make superficial judgements on people — as, alas, church bodies constantly do — without going to the necessary trouble of trying to understand, as God does, what lies behind the outward behaviour and what that behaviour means. There is no "slide rule" way of evaluating human behaviour. What is a serious "sin" for one may, to another elsewhere on the road to grace, be a sad, but comparatively trivial, lapse. It all depends on the perspective from which you look and the understanding which you have.

This attribute, the divine understanding, is truly one that makes for healing. We may hide our faults and feelings from our friends and fear the disillusionment that must surely, we anticipate, follow their discovery. God is in a different position. He is, as John told us above, "well aware of what human nature is like." It is out of his understanding of us in our totality that healing can begin. As the comedienne, Hylda Baker, used to say in quite another context: "He knows, you know." He does!

Awareness of that divine understanding which sees our worst before others do, and even before we ourselves do, might at first, seem a counsel of despair. It is, in fact, the reverse. Healing begins from the knowledge that all we are and do is accepted in the divine understanding. What goes wrong repeatedly for us is seen by him in true perspective and can even be made the ground of our new being.

The Divine Sensitivity

Very close to this is divine sensitivity to our needs. That sensitivity is, again, an attribute we see so clearly in the Healing Word, the Logos, Jesus Christ. The Gospel record is full of the sensitivity of Christ. "Sheep without a shepherd" secured his attention, even though he had retired to quietness. Children and parents rebuked by the disciples, heard him saying: "Suffer the little children to come unto me, and forbid them not." Perhaps that sensitivity is stated supremely in the re-assuring statement that "he knows our needs *before* we ask."

In human relationships sensitivity is a requirement of any who seek to offer healing. It is a word that speaks of (in the best sense) subtlety, sure-ness of touch, sympathy. It is a concept that lays importance on empathy and intuition. Sensitivity is founded on respect for personality, so there will never be invasion of privacy, but it also has a prophetic or at least anticipatory quality — that enables the healing agent to sense need, despair, guilt in advance. This allows that care-full concern that is recognisable as response to need, a response which will not be turned into words or actions until the right time for that has come.

That which we see happening, at one level, in human relationships, is increased a hundred per cent at the divine level. The sensitivity of God is as real as the remarkable sensitivity demonstrated by Jesus in his life on earth. When the rich young ruler could not face the cost of discipleship, as we have noted earlier, no pressure came from Christ to keep him there. Sadly, but with sensitivity, he let him go. When that "woman of bad reputation" crept quietly into the company gathered for a meal in the Pharisee's house, the sensitivity of Christ enabled him to receive graciously and indeed gratefully, the spontaneous love of a woman of moral weakness so far as official religion was concerned, but who had intense sincerity. She was therefore, in the eyes of Christ, and in the understanding of God, more in touch with true spiritual reality than a correct but cold Simon, the Pharisee. When a puzzled "Master of Israel", Nicodemus, came by night to see him, Jesus did not upbraid him for the dishonesty of clandestine conversations, but saw him as a seeker after truth, and led him towards it.

I remember once, some years ago, watching with anxiety the pain and struggle of someone who had decided to tell me of a situation so far not made known to me in case it resulted in criticism or even, more likely, total rejection . The fact that, although up to that moment I had not consciously considered what might be taking place in that life that would create anxiety, I was nevertheless able to anticipate first the general area of concern and then, still in advance, name the reason for that concern simply took all the pressure out of that problem. My stating what the reasons for the anxiety were brought an immediate transformation. What had been an area of dread and had been associated with possible disillusionment on my part and a diminution of my respect for that person, was now seen to involve acceptance in place of rejection and goodwill, not hostility.

Multiplied infinitely and caught up in the timelessness of God, it is exactly the same with the divine sensitivity. Our sins are no surprise to God! As a result of this fore-knowledge, our attitude in prayer is completely changed. When we "take it to the Lord in prayer" (as the old hymn says), we are not there to give news bulletins of information as yet unproclaimed. We are there to recognise that God, knowing all, does not break the relationship because of what he knows. Rather he renews it and strengthens it.

Can there be an attribute of the Logos, the Healing Word, that ministers more to our comfort and assurance than the divine sensitivity, so demonstrated as a reality in the life of the Christ, the Healer? I think the answer to that must be "No." So, again I say it, the foreknowledge of God, sometimes presented as a matter for fear and trembling is, in fact, the most re-assuring knowledge ever. Yes, he knows, you know!

Chapter 17

The Divine Empathy

"Jesus, the Son of God ... is not a high priest who is unable to sympathise with the weaknesses we possess ... in every respect (he) has gone through the same ordeal of temptation as we have to go through ..." (Hebrews 4:15 *WB*).

That verse is a statement of the divine empathy in all its wonder and glory. What a healing attribute the Logos, the Healing Word presents! This is indeed love in action. That our weaknesses and failures should touch such a chord in the realms of the divine is good news, Gospel, indeed! There must be joy in every human heart when it can be seen that our ways, though not God's ways, are understood and sympathetically felt in the heart of God. He "feels" as well as knows.

In speaking in this way, it may sometimes seem as if I am speaking very anthropomorphically and, in terms of intellectual academic approaches, naïvely. I accept this, but I repeat that my purpose is primarily pastoral and designed to try to help every Christian, at whatever level they function, to touch the great theological truths behind the language I use to create that recognition. The verse which I quoted from Hebrews at the beginning of this reflection is the statement of a great and profound theological truth — the fact that because of the Incarnation of Christ, and his fully human life in the world, there is real empathy within the right relationship made possible in Christ, through the Spirit, on the Father's initiative. That is theological reality. It is also the reality of Christian experience. So while some of the ways in which I say these things may feel romantic to the strictly intellectual mind, I am making known to ordinary Christians the truths that relate to our experience of God's love, made known in Christ, and wholly confirmed objectively in the witness of the Word of God.

It is the experience of every pastor in relation to his people
that temptation, acceding to temptation and therefore feeling
guilty so often brings to the devoted Christian, agony of soul.

> Wilt thou forgive that sinne where I begunne,
> Which is my sin, though it were done before?
> Wilt thou forgive those sinnes, through which I runne,
> And do run still: though still I do deplore?
> When thou hast done, thou hast not done,
> For I have more.

> Wilt thou forgive that sinne by which I'have wonne
> Others to sinne? and made my sin their door?
> Wilt thou forgive that sinne which I did shunne
> A yeare, or two: but wallowed in a score?
> When thou has done, thou has not done,
> For I have more.

How easy it is to empathise with John Donne's words as he
looks into his life and soul, for there is every one of us! Guilt
is, as every pastor knows and as has been already stated, the
bug-bear of so many, yet guilt there should be. It is not only
right but necessary to feel guilt when we fall short of
standards. Not to feel guilty over wrong done reminds of that
blindness I talked of as characterising the Pharisees to whom
Jesus issued the extreme warning about the possibility of an
"unforgivable sin." Appropriate guilt is proper. What ought to
concern the pastor is guilt which is out of all proportion to
fault and which persists, unhealed, even when forgiveness has
been assured. That guilt is inappropriate and cries out for
further help and understanding.

Setting aside the complex problems of a guilt that is
pathological — for digression into a full understanding of the
psychological factors that can play a part in such guilt would
require a scope and depth of treatment that is inappropriate
here — we must still face, realistically, the agony and despair
which a true and proper guilt can bring, despair which all the
greatest saints have known so fully. The more sensitive a soul

is to having "sinned against God", the greater the level of spiritual agony can be. Have we "crucified the Son of God afresh and put him to an open shame?" (Hebrews 6:6). The hurt felt by those who are on the road of sanctification yet fail, is deep. "Wave upon wave of grace" (*John 1:16 WB*) is necessary to see us through it.

It is here that a sense of the reality of the divine empathy brings healing. Temptation is not peculiar to us. Sin is common to all mankind for (as I quoted earlier) "all have sinned and come short of the glory of God." But the point I am making in this reflection is that — yes, it can be said — temptation is also part of the divine experience — in as real a way as possible. The sins felt and faced by God-made-man were not so much the ones that trouble humanity most ... such as sins of behaviour in relationship whether of a sexual, bitter, or unrighteously angry kind (for example). The focal point of the Devil's attack on Christ was the use of power, the divine and special power Jesus recognised to be God's gift to him, the "beloved Son in whom (God) was well-pleased" (Matthew 3:17). Should he use it for material ends (stones into bread)? Should he perform divine conjuring tricks (like jumping off the temple tower)? Should he be a military Messiah and conquer the kingdoms of the world? Nor was that "attack" temporary. "The devil left him for a season" (Luke 4:13). He returned at all the crucial points in Jesus' life. He was present in Gethsemane ("Let this cup pass from me"). He was active on Calvary ("My God, my God, why hast thou forsaken me?") Whether temptation is to be explained in terms of a personal power to be called Satan or, as others would prefer, as the inner pressures that well up inside and come from the negative or shadow side of our personal and collective unconscious, or whether indeed there is something of both realities, the interplay of psychic negative forces and powers (the cosmic principalities and powers of darkness of which — or whom — St Paul was aware), the basic experience is the same. There is the pressure from within to accede to the promptings of the dark side; there is the struggle during the sinning; there is the regret and remorse afterwards. Whether it be temper lost, bitterness expressed, failure of a "physical" kind, denial, betrayal, destruction of trust, "internal" dishonesty or "external" degradation, sincere misunderstanding, deliberate self-delusion, the feelings are the same. The agony of remorse drove Peter to tears and Judas Iscariot to suicide. How easily that awful realisation that comes when temptation has passed and sin is complete can drive the troubled soul to agony and despair. Go on with John Donne, but go right to the end:

> I have a sinne of feare, that when I have spunne
> My last thred, I shall perish on the shore;
> Sweare by thy selfe, that at my death thy sonne
> Shall shine as he shines now, and heretofore;
> And, having done that, Thou haste done,
> *I feare no more.*

Behind the divine empathy, there is the divine consistency. That means the understanding of God, through Christ's experience, becomes the forgiveness of God "until seventy-times seven."

The divine empathy is so supremely an attribute of the Healing Word, who is Christ, that it must be reflected in the pastor and in the church as a whole. The faults that are found in the people of God must be understood in every way possible by the pastors who minister to them. Above all, (as I have already quoted) the important words that remind us that "God sent not his Son into the world to condemn the world" but that it might be saved through him, must take the pastor into a deep understanding of the things that go wrong in the life of the believer and how this comes to be so. But there is more. The pastor too is human — a fact "the church" does not always acknowledge. He/she also has wrestled in agony with temptation. He/she too has "gone under" repeatedly ("for I have more"). He/she too has known the remorse, the regret, the agony of failure, perhaps all the more because of his/her special position. The church, sharing the divine empathy, must allow for human failure more than it sometimes does.

It is worrying to see, sometimes, the harshness of judgement and attitude that "the church" from time to time shows to those who wrestle with temptation but fail, for such a judgemental and rigid attitude can never reflect the God who is love, and has shown it in Christ. Let those who are called to pastoral ministry for ever dwell on that awe-inspiring phrase already quoted: "There but for the grace of God, go I." And if indeed they have gone through the fire themselves, through the grace of God, they will have learned the full meaning of the attribute of empathy and its part in the healing of people. And the empathy they have learned will reflect, in some small way, the empathy which is divine and is so much part of the Healing Word.

Chapter 18

The Divine Compassion

Behind all healing attitudes, there lies compassion. Nowhere is this divine attribute described more beautifully than in the phrase "moved with compassion", which somehow sums up the very heart of the divine purpose. "God so loved the world that he gave his only begotten Son that whosoever believeth on him should not perish . . ." The redemption of the world takes place on the divine initiative — "who first loved us." The Incarnation, like the cross, could only happen because of the divine compassion. The Messiah, "given" in such a context, was often "moved with compassion." "And Jesus, moved with compassion . . . put forth his hand." "When he saw the multitudes, he was moved with compassion on them . . ."

Efforts made to very this phrase in other translations fail to catch the wonder of this, the divine attitude as "moved with compassion" does. "With warm indignation" in the *New English Bible* version falls short. The second verse I quoted above sounds a little better — "moved to pity." That last phrase and "he had compassion" are the *Revised Standard Version* renderings. "He felt sorry" and "feeling sorry" are the contributions of the *Jerusalem Bible*. "Filled with pity" and "deeply moved with pity" come from J. B. Phillips.

In the end I go back to that *Authorised Version* translation of so long ago as the most inspired of all. Jesus was "moved with compassion." That phrase says almost everything that needs to be said about the nature of God.

Compassion is, by derivation, a "suffering with" someone, yet it is a quality that is more than sympathy or even empathy, both of which might well be described as involving compassion — which they do. These words, particularly and more specifically empathy, speak of understanding and, as far as possible, actual sharing of suffering in "feeling" terms, but we still have to recognise that there are limits to our ability to feel realistically just what the sufferer feels. The pain someone bears is, and can only be, *their* pain. To enter into it and feel it

---

*I have made this point in the discussion of "Compassion" as a "fruit of the Spirit" in CREATIVE SILENCE (pp. 109-111).

as they feel it, lies beyond our normal human ability. The thoughts and feelings of those who are incurably ill, draw forth our sympathy and our sincere attempts at empathy, but it is not easy and perhaps not possible for the sympathiser to feel just what being in that position does to attitudes, relationships and ways of living. Compassion goes one step further than sympathy or empathy usually do, just because there is the element of being "moved" deeply within it. In compassion, we are compelled to take some action, however limited that action can be. In the case of the sick man mentioned in the first of my quotations at the beginning of this chapter, Jesus actually "stretched out his hand and touched him." The leper was cleansed. In the case of the multitudes referred to in the second quotation, Jesus responded by appointing disciples "to cast out devils and to cure every kind of ailment and disease." Compassion results in action of some kind . . . a touch, an embrace, a kiss, a decision . . . because the inner heart has been "moved."

The feeling of compassion welling up is a distinctive one and a recognisable one. It happens in situations that, for some reason not necessarily definable, have the capacity to touch the deep places, to graze the soul, to create love. The feelings are subjective, but their compassionate characteristic is their objectivity. This is not the love that identifies in a way that brings "emotional involvement." It is not the love that moves on to a relationship of shorter or longer duration. It is the outflow of the moment, in response to need or pain, bereavement or hurt. Sincerely offered, it brings the blessing of the moment. Having given from the soul in that moment whatever action has been felt appropriate, we move on to the next thing we have to do, the next moment that may move us to compassion again.

Our moments of compassion may come seldom or often, but when they do, they are expressing something which is, by nature, a manifestation of the healing heart of God.

Let us be glad when we are "moved to compassion." It is a sign of the presence of the healing Spirit within us.

Chapter 19

Healing Distance

It may well come as a surprise to find a chapter headed "Healing Distance" for what possibility is there that distance could be an attitude of the Healing Word, Jesus? After all, the symbols of healing are the out-stretched hands, the open arms, the loving embrace, the caring touch, etc. There is however within healing processes, also at times, the need for distance. As there is some evidence of it being used to help people to be whole in the attitude of the Healing Word, Jesus Christ, the Incarnate Logos of God, it is worth testing out this concept by looking at some parts of his ministry.

There were times when Jesus, very consciously and very deliberately, kept his distance — both from situations and from people. I am not referring to times when he needed to "retreat", which he did periodically. True, he did put distance between himself and the people crying out for him, for a time. I am thinking more of instances like that involving the rich young ruler and the death of Lazarus. In both these cases, Jesus "set boundaries" in order to do what was ultimately of a healing nature.

The story of the rich young ruler is a striking example of the need to allow "space" to someone seeking the wholeness of being that is healing. There is no doubt that the young nobleman was a man truly seeking after truth and Jesus recognised this. He was a young man for whom Jesus felt a real admiration and affection: a man of real honesty. For all these reasons, Jesus "beholding him, loved him" (Mark 10:21).

Where such feelings are present, the natural attitude would understandably have been closeness. But Jesus kept his distance and put to him — as he asked — the demands of the Kingdom. He then gave him the space to refuse those demands and allowed him to go away. There was no restraining hand, no persuasion: "Don't go, look at it this way." Jesus recognised that what this good young man did need at that time was to distance himself and see, from a longer perspective, what he was being asked to do.

It is, in the same sense that the parable of the prodigal son was concerned with "space" and "distance." The only way for the young man to "come to himself" was by going to a "far country." Healing involved first distance and then return. Real freedom of choice is needed to create true commitment. We must never invade the privacy of personality where a free choice is to be made. This is the way God acts towards people. We are not puppets on a string manipulated into the Kingdom against our will. That is not the way God deals with people. All who are involved in the work of evangelism should remember the basic principles of healing relationship spelt out so clearly in the parable of the prodigal son.

The other situation of which I am thinking — that concerning Lazarus' death — is quite extraordinary. The same features are there but the point is made much more dramatically. The passage I refer to is in John, chapter 11. It describes a situation and a set of relationships that are full of love. Jesus *loved* Lazarus. "Lord", said Martha and Mary, *"he whom thou lovest* is sick." "Now Jesus *loved* Martha and her sister and Lazarus." So you would expect in such a situation that a loving Christ, disturbed by the news of illness in the family and especially when it involved Lazarus, would "make haste" to Bethany, anxious to heal Lazarus and allay the fears and worries of Martha and Mary. But he did not do so. He took the extraordinary step of remaining at a distance from the distressing situation — a distance of "fifteen furlongs."

That one who might have saved the life of a beloved friend and who could have comforted two other people important to him, should, with calm deliberation, decline to go and do it, seems, by any standard, heartless in the extreme. But Jesus kept his distance. "Lord, if thou hadst been here, my brother had not died", said Martha. "Lord, if thou hadst been here, my brother had not died", said a weeping Mary, prostrate at his feet.

Jesus wept.

He was not heartless.

But he kept his distance.

The distance Jesus created was the space needed for a miracle. The greater ministry, the long-term healing demanded, even if it went to more than four days (as Martha pointed out), time, space and distance.

All that lies behind and within this story is beyond the purpose of these reflections, but the way Jesus used distance and space is a lesson we should not ignore, especially if we are impetuous in relationship and tend to swamp those with whom we have to do, people who are overwhelmed unhelpfully by a love that knows no boundaries or bounds.

Personality is sacred. Privacy is a right. Our secrets are our own until *we* choose to reveal them. In our relationship to others, we shall use healing closeness if that seems appropriate to us, but it may be necessary for us to remember the place of distance in healing ministry.

Distance and Inner Strength

Those who are called to reflect the Logos, Christ, the Healing Word, need to draw their strength and energy from him. It might be — but it is not always so in reality — that those who are involved in caring should have access to care and support themselves. In the social service and counselling professions, it is normal to have a supervision or support group to meet this need. The pastor, clerical or lay, is so often on his or her own. The parish priest often ends the day alone, duties done, ministry effected, masses conducted and the masses helped, alone. So often those who minister are thrown back on their own resources, the inner resources of their own faith and strength.

This is a pastoral responsibility that is carried over the years by so many. Sometimes it is effected with quiet success. Others break under it. The church however is not always ready, as I said earlier, to acknowledge that its servants are human and weak and will fail. The space to acknowledge human weakness and fault is not always given to its servants by the officially compassionate church of the truly compassionate Christ. If the pastor must walk alone, drawing on his or her own inner resources (and Paul's statement about "inner resources" in the *New English Bible* is relevant here for he says he has learnt "whatever the circumstances" to draw upon "resources in himself", Philippians 4:11) then that servant of Christ will gain greatly from seeing how Jesus maintained his own inner calm and serenity, whatsoever the pressures. He had his friends, male and female, of course. He had his disciples. But there was an area — the hidden area over which Mary "pondered" so often "in her heart", in which he lived alone. No one else could enter it and understand it. It belonged to the inner silence of his own soul.

Whatever any one of us may carry is much less than he did, but the pattern is common to all in pastoral ministry and service. "Go into your room and close your door." The inner world is the place of secrets and no one has a right to invade it arrogantly or subtly, without permission. It is in that realm of profound and secret thought — and feeling — that the test of the healing attribute comes, for it is there that anything from disappointment to heartbreak will impinge on life. It was in the inner recesses that our Lord must have felt the desolation of the betrayal, the denial and the unanimous act of forsaking and fleeing which afflicted frightened men ("the disciples all forsook him and fled" — Matthew 26:56).

It would have been so easy and — in terms of human nature, as one knows it — natural for each of these situations to bring bitterness and resentment but Christ being the man he was, did not allow them to do so. The healing attitude which Christ was able to maintain, no matter what happened to him personally, was a divine attribute, hard for any of us to emulate.

The denying Peter was the rock on which the church could be built. The slumbering disciples in Gethsemane were, after the coming of Pentecost, wide-awake to the demands of the Kingdom. The men who did forsake him and flee were, in the end, willing to stand for him, even at the cost of life itself. Bitterness in the face of public denial, personal betrayal and man's desertion would surely have been the reaction of us all to such treatment, yet Christ was able to maintain his healing attitude even in such desperate circumstances. He was indeed the Healing Word.

If we have been called to ministry, ordained or lay, we have this sort of test to face, something of this success to find. It is not the ability to maintain a healing attitude when all is well that is the test of grace. It is the ability to love under pressure, to be reconciling in the face of derision and hostility, to be healing when that which creates bitterness or those who are hostile are present. This is the demand of the Gospel. The example is Christ. The call is to remain the healing pastor against personal odds and through personal crisis.

Perhaps the concept of healing distance is not irrelevant here, as it holds one clue to success in this effort of grace, When Peter denied Christ, he was following "afar-off" — at a distance. In Gethsemane, Jesus told the disciples to sit "here while I go and pray yonder" at a distance. The prodigal son, as I noted earlier, went to a far country in order to discover the relationship that mattered. Somewhere in all this, there is something that must be heard. It was at the end of the journey to Emmaus that the two disciples recognised their Lord. Perhaps one clue to the ability to maintain a healing attitude is to hold people at the right distance. Perhaps the clue to finding healing is, sometimes, to accept distance. Perhaps the ability to maintain calm under stress is not unrelated to the idea of distance too.

Chapter 20

The Indwelling Christ

The root, source and basis of any healing attribute we may have or any healing attitudes reflected in us and through us, can only be one, so far as Christians are concerned. It lies in our union, in the Spirit, with the Logos, Love, the Healing Word, Christ. The source of our Lord's own ability to minister as he did, he places firmly in his own union with God, his unity in God. "I am not myself the source of the words that I speak unto you", he says (John 14:10–11, *NEB*); "it is the Father who dwells in me doing his own work." He points to the "evidence of the deeds themselves" as the sign that "I am in my Father and the Father in me." He then goes on to make the extraordinary pronouncement (verse 12): "In truth, in very truth, I tell you, he who has faith in me will do what I am doing, and he will do greater things still because I am going to the Father." So in verses 13–14, the promises are made: "Indeed anything you ask in my name, I will do so that the Father may be glorified in the Son. If you ask anything in my name, I will do it."

The passage, like the promises, are not easy for would-be disciples. Our experience so often is that miracles do not happen and the reasons for failure are not obvious. "If my love were but more simple, I would take him at his word" says the hymn. There are many times when simple faith is not justified (so far as we can understand, at least through a glass darkly) by the miracles we seek but do not see, and disillusionment comes. Was there not enough faith? But we know there could not have been more. Or could there have been. . .? Is it our sin that is getting the way? Are we not spiritual enough? Is it that our finite sight cannot see the miracles that are coming in a way we do not understand — or want? We just do not understand. "God moves in a mysterious way his wonders to perform."

There is no question that, over and over again, Christians come face to face with the cruel doubt that that experience brings. And that doubt must be honoured. We did ask "in his name." We did ask "anything in his name." But nothing happened.

The basis for our healing attitudes is entrenched in the authority of Christ. In matters of a spiritual nature Christ spoke from a depth that no one else has ever known. That is a judgement that may be disputed but the intuition of the ages, from outside Christianity as well as within, is that he had such authority. Christ was a master of the spiritual life and spoke with knowledge. He himself — if the Gospels are accepted as giving a realistic assessment of him both on facts and in comment — was absolutely categorical on why he had authority in such matters. He lived in such a relationship to God that he *knew*. "If you knew me, you would know my Father too" (John 14:7 *NEB*). That is a stupendous claim! We may avoid it by deciding that John's Gospel, written so long after Jesus' death, was an interpretation of his teaching rather than a report of it. It is not easy however to imagine any disciple — not least one who "at supper" had "leaned back close to him" (John 21:20, *NEB*) — inventing a relationship of this kind and depth or having an understanding of the relationship that John 14 expounds so fully and so specifically. I therefore find myself with no alternative but to return, in my search for healing attitudes, to the authority of our Lord in this field and to seek to understand more of the miracles that he made clear would happen "in his name."

God's purpose for us is that we should be "truly well." That means that it is our wholeness — in "body, soul, mind and spirit" — that is his concern. Perhaps it is that our view of the miracles we seek is too limited at times to see that it is not just "physical" healing that is our need.

That is easy to say when one has been blessed with health. To the sufferer who seeks deliverance from serious or even mortal illness of the body, it does not always come as the comfort sought. But it remains a concept that we have to ponder so that we can see our true well-being in perspective and come nearer to understanding the spiritual laws and principles at work in the ministry of the Healing Word.

Let us look then a little further at the relationship Jesus claims with the Father for it is the source of the power he demonstrates and the love he is able to express even in very negative circumstances.

Just as Christ's word and work were not done of himself but because of his Father "who dwelleth in me" (John 14:10), so any healing propensity in us comes wholly through the indwelling Christ. He is the source of our healing attitudes. His presence within us creates compassion. We can know the Spirit for "he dwelleth with you and shall be in you."

The concept of Christ as *in* the disciple and, as Paul stresses, the disciple being *in* Christ, is fundamental to our growth in grace and gifts and fruits. Jesus expounds the relationship in terms of the vine, in the fifteenth chapter of John's Gospel. The central, focal point in the use of the vine as a symbol of being "in Christ" is the repeated emphasis on *the impossibility of fruit without Christ*, the vine itself. "It is essential that you should remain in me and I in you. No branch can bear fruit in isolation by itself: it must remain in the vine: you are the branches" (William Barclay's translation).

Statements like this are either extraordinarily arrogant or born out of such conviction that they are absolutely authoritative. There may be, as I said above, questions as to the nature of John's Gospel — is it reported statement or interpretation of statements or in modern journalistic terms, fact or comment? The Gospel was written so long after the earthly life of our Lord closed that technical questions about the content of John's record have inevitably been raised. To go into these matters is the purpose of New Testament scholarship and lies outside the content of these reflections.

What is so extraordinary is what J. B. Phillips calls, in a famous phrase, "the ring of truth." For many they may be inspired invention or interpretation. I simply acknowledge that "ring of truth" and hear our Lord himself speaking through the words.

Christ's inner convictions were the product of very specific events and not just subjective phantasy of the "delusions of grandeur" kind. For him the baptism was as objective as any experience could be just as the immediately following experience of temptation was too. Everything he sensed and experienced, when tested against the prophecies of the Old Testament, pointed to his being the "beloved Son" in whom God was "well pleased." The word "must" that he uses so often to describe what he is or will do testifies to that inner certainty and conviction which gives him his authority. From his earliest years, he "*must* be about his Father's business." In his later (in terms of his short life) years, he *must* go to Jerusalem and "suffer many things of the elders and chief priests and scribes, and be killed and be raised again the third day" (Matthew 16:21). "The Son of Man *must* be lifted up so that whosoever believeth in him should not perish, but have everlasting life" (John 3:14–15).

That authority granted to Jesus, the emphasis he put on himself as "in" us as the basis of all we are and do, must be taken seriously. He *is* the basis, source and root of all we seek to become. Similarly he is the fount of all the church's energy, power and life. Too often the church pursuing a necessary emphasis with enthusiasm — social outreach for example — is in danger of losing contact with its source. That is why a caring church always runs the risk of becoming simply social service. The servant church needs to remain close to the cosmic Christ if it would fulfil its *Christian* task. The Christian is called, as Christians are, to be involved in politics, education, economics, the arts, psychological and psychiatric understanding, etc., but none of these tasks can be served properly if the link between expertise and Christ as Lord of all life, is broken. "Without me, you can do nothing."

Withered branches are, in the end, signs of death and dying and proclaim that life is no longer present in roots and trunk or stem. "Abide in me and I in you. As the branch cannot bear fruit of itself, except it abide in the vine, no more can ye, except ye abide in me. I am the vine, ye are the branches."

The source of all our healing attributes and attitudes is very clear. It is a Christ-centred, Christ-based faith: in the Christ, the Logos, in the Healing Word, Love, who dwells within us.

PART III

HEALING WORDS

Chapter 21

Forgiveness

I turn finally to some of the great, as I would call them, "healing words" of the Bible. All of them have meaning and content only in relation to the Healing Word, Jesus Christ, the Logos, Love. That said, reflection on some of these words will bring blessing, comfort and grace.

Words are the medium through which ideas are expressed. Despite the reaction against "verbal" processes as means of communication, especially in those areas which put so much — and sometimes too much emphasis — on feeling, "non-verbal communication" and "body language", words will continue to be our essential method of communication. I have, in this book, made central the Healing *Word* which "became flesh and dwelt among us." The great healing *words* come from and through the Word of God Incarnate.

"Take with you words" said the prophet Hosea. Stricken, sad, sorrowing humanity needs words of healing. There are words that can redeem the agony of doubt, the anguish of sin, the anxiety of fear; words that can meet, intellectually, the most profound thinking that man can offer: words that can minister to the most disturbed of emotions; words that can bring peace where there is no peace; words of assurance and re-assurance, of forgiveness and renewal, of the security of acceptance and the encouragement to achievement. Words can be instruments of peace, an orchestration of joy, a symphony of the sounds of salvation. Through words, Christ is made known. Through healing words, the grace of the Lord Jesus Christ can come in benediction.

Down through the ages the prophets proclaimed the words of God. "These are the words of the Lord God" Ezekiel said so constantly and, through those words, God was the more known. Through words, we can reach and touch the very nature of truth and the very core of life.

Of all the healing words of the New Testment the word *forgiveness* must take first place, for it is the centrality of the doctrine of forgiveness that determines the nature of the Christian Gospel.

If "love casts out fear", forgiveness equally casts out guilt — or will do so if we allow that to happen, not holding on defiantly, consciously or unconsciously to our guilt. The disease and the dis-comfort guilt brings can only be dissipated totally when we understand and are able to accept the great credal statement: "I believe in the forgiveness of sins."

Forgiveness is the free act of God, in grace, in restoring our relationship with him through setting aside our failures of love. The power those failures had or might have over us is gone. It is at the very heart of the Christian Gospel that it is through the divine initiative the offer of forgiveness and restored relationship is made possible. It *is* the Christian Gospel that God took those steps in the Incarnation, Death and Resurrection of Christ. Forgiveness is dependent on nothing other than the acceptance of grace. "Immortal love, for ever full, for ever flowing free", we sing. It is. So Professor James Atkinson writes in the *Dictionary of Christian Theology* edited by Alan Richardson (SCM Press): "We should resist the prevalent psychological attempts to explain the divine relationship as consequent upon human thoughts, feelings, acts . . . it is not biblical teaching."

The point is a crucially important one, for as Reformed theology so dramatically and rightly insisted, forgiveness is of *grace alone*. We cannot earn it, deserve it, or claim it by anything we have to offer. All we can do is gratefully and graciously receive it. It is there and available. Our need of it is, as I have noted earlier, known "before we ask." "Nothing in our hands we bring, simply to Thy Cross we cling" is the old evangelical expression of it in the hymn, Rock of Ages. The language is unimportant. It is the reality that matters. Not by what we do, but by what God has done in Christ, is there "forgiveness of sins."

We can take the point even as far as saying that

forgiveness is not dependent on repentance. The sense of repentance that we feel is *our response to the enormity of the offer made.* "Love so amazing, so divine, demands my soul, my life, my all." "Love calls out repentance from the human heart" (to quote Atkinson again), "as the sun brings new life out of a plant." The teaching on forgiveness must always be safeguarded against any idea that repentance is the human contribution to the bargain. We are not talking of a new relationship that is the product of human actions — like a treaty between nations, or a contract between individuals. We are speaking of a restored opportunity for fellowship with God that has been created by him alone. It is neither merited nor deserved.

What I have been stating is a theological proposition which is, as I understand it, true. It can only be "believed" if, through individual experience, each finds it to be true in their own spiritual lives. And just this has been the experience of "forgiveness" of people down the ages as they contemplated that God who "so loved the world." It is acknowledgement not attainment that "leads to life." It is the act of receiving, not the fact of deserving, that restores relationship. This is the Gospel, the Good News to sorely troubled, guilt-laden souls who seek for inner peace. It is not in the strain and stress of spiritual struggle against the odds, nor is it in the need to please, to satisfy some Divine potentate, that salvation lies. *It is in the acceptance of a gift.* So our deep and proper sense of penitence, regret, remorse, shame, all feelings appropriate to the sense of guilt, are products of the forgiveness offered, not the reason for its having been given.

I have said something of appropriate and inappropriate or pathological guilt in chapter 17. I take the theme up again here. It is so much part of the ministry of the Church to bring ease to the guilty that something more needs to be said on it than I have said so far.

One of the most heartfelt and moving cries for the healing

word of forgiveness is contained in Psalm 51. Traditionally this Psalm has been linked with David's penitence after his adultery with Bathsheba, the wife of Uriah, the Hittite. Perhaps the worst part of that sin was not the actual adultery itself, but the deliberate sending of Uriah, a commander in David's army, to "the front" to ensure the likelihood of his death. That was a cold, calculated use of power for selfish ends. Scholarship would not necessarily defend the link between the Psalm and David, but in terms of human understanding, the link is a helpful one.

This is a case when an acute sense of guilt is wholly appropriate and the cry for forgiveness right and proper: "Wash away all my guilt and cleanse me from my sin ... Turn thy face from my sins and blot out all my guilt ... Create a pure heart in me."

The first grace in such a situation is to see the reality and degree of failure, the second to acknowledge it and the third to seek forgiveness of it. Confession has therefore been a normal part of Christian worship and in some branches of the Church, of church discipline.

The ministry of Word and Sacrament must allow an opportunity in worship for all present to have the time and context available to allow a real awareness of regret for specific failures and space to ask for and receive the forgiveness always promised. The nature of "confession" prayers offered sometimes fails to touch need and longing because of their personal irrelevance. We have not all, always, "failed miserably" or failed in *everything*. General statements of failure are appropriate and helpful, for (for example) "we have all sinned in thought and word and deed." Time to be aware of specific thoughts, words and deeds needs to be allowed to let the statement "ring true", at both the conscious and the unconscious levels. Consciously we are, if we are honest with ourselves, always aware where we have done or been wrong. Sometimes we are also dimly aware of the unconscious ways in which we fail and which Paul referred to in that Romans 7 passage. I draw attention to this passage so often because it is so important. Indeed, at the risk of irritating some readers, I will quote it in full again, in the *New English Bible* version:

"The will to do good is there, the deed is not. The good which I want to do, I fail to do; but what I do is the wrong which is against my will; and if what I do is against my will, clearly it is no longer I who am the agent, but sin that has its lodging in me. I discover this principle then: that when I want to do the right, only the wrong is within my reach. In my inmost self I delight in the law of God, but I perceive that there is in my bodily members a different law, fighting against the law that my reason approves and making me a prisoner under the law that is in my members, the law of sin. Miserable creature that I am, who is there to rescue me out of this body doomed to death? God alone, through Jesus Christ our Lord! Thanks be to God! In a word then, I myself, subject to God's law as a rational being, am yet, in my unspiritual nature, a slave to the law of sin."

There are many in the psychological and associated fields who will see in this profound statement some kind of neurotic guilt consciousness not admired by modern people. In other words, they might be willing to see the validity or appropriateness of a sense of guilt that relates to "guilt-worthy" (if I may coin a word) happenings. What they would question is its appropriateness to a *state* rather than to particular actions. I believe, in fact, that it is both a profound and a true Christian insight to be aware of both *sins* and *sin,* for both "sins" as events and "sin" as a state must be brought into our confession and the realm of forgiveness.

There is a corporate psychic negativity within the life and soul of mankind that demands the redemptive activity of God at both conscious and unconscious levels. In terms of evangelism, there is no defence for any approach that plays on the deep guilt feelings, latent or potent, below the surface of consciousness — and most emotionally-orientated evangelism does just that. It *is* necessary that we enable

people to *be* aware of conscious fault and to *become* aware of
the responsibility for unconscious guilt feelings, a result of
the "collective shadow" that is a reality of life. It is wrong to
play on the fear element in such guilt.

It is within this context that we can look at the important
phrase "The Healing of the Memories."* It is in that very
realm of conscious and unconscious memory that this
concept so applies. We remember a great deal, but within the
memory there are boundaries that make themselves known as
we try to recall material from the past. In fact we remember
everything that has ever happened to us. What we cannot do
is *recall* everything. It is here, once again, that we meet these
now familiar concepts of "conscious" and "unconscious".
There is much that can be remembered and recalled
consciously and we have to deal with that material in a way
appropriate to it. Our bigger problems lie with that material
which is part of us, but which is "unconscious" — all the good
and bad experiences of life from its beginning. In this
connection, we are like computers. Everything has been "fed
in" to memory. What we cannot do is recall all of it and
especially those early unhappy experiences which we have
repressed because we could not face the memory of them.
Through therapy, hypnosis, dreams, analysis, primal therapy
it is possible to come into touch with some of those memories,
but a vast number remain unrecalled. Some will cause us
discomfort, dis-ease and pain. Some may express themselves
in psychosomatic illness. There are memories that need to be
healed through forgiveness, so that they are "remembered no
more." That is not possible for they are part of us, but what
they lose is their power to hurt and to harm. Then are the
memories truly healed. Conscious memories that we have
feared have no more capacity to hurt us. The process of
forgiveness has taken place. The handing over of our
unconscious selves to God is an act of faith. We ask to be
made aware of what we should know in order to face and
accept it so that its redemption may follow. What we can
never know, we entrust to him. Grace permeates down

*See also Appendix

through our whole being to bring forgiveness and therefore healing in the deepest places. The unhealed memory that hurts will work against us, but the hurtful memory redeemed will work for us.

It is here perhaps that the sacrament of the Lord's Supper is so relevant. "This do in remembrance of me", or, as William Barclay puts it: "You must continue to do this to make you remember me" (I Corinthians 11:24). This search for the healing of the memories ends at the table of the Lord, for there the source of grace is made real. The Sacrament is not merely a memorial. It is a means of grace. *There* is the memory that heals.

Forgiveness is the healing word where there is healthy, realistic and appropriate guilt and every act of worship must make real the sense of "wiping out" and of removal that the credal statement about forgiveness brings. The "guilty" soul needs to sense and feel the unlimited nature of forgiveness in its scope, outreach and regenerating power. That is the great reality of Christian belief and of Christian experience.

Forgiveness, as a healing word, is timeless. However far in the past failure lies, all is made new. Forgiveness covers the healing of all memories, the healing of the here and now, and the healing of the future. For all meet the forgiving God in Christ in the eternal now. The forgiveness of sins is always available. It has no limitations of time or space. It is God's nature to want us to be made whole and that purpose never changes. It is his promise to forgive, forgive and forgive again. There is no power of evil strong enough to defeat his ultimate love.

Forgiveness is then the most profound of healing words, a word the guilty must readily receive, hold and cherish.

Chapter 22

Redemption

The word *redemption* is one of the most healing words in the Bible. It whispers of sin forgiven. It speaks of new opportunity. It sings of freedom. It shouts hope.

There are a number of words in the Christian vocabulary that have been confined and narrowed by association with particular approaches related to the evangelical crusade and mission hall style of proclamation, thus linking them mainly to "conservative" and "fundamentalist" ways of proclaiming the Gospel. "Salvation", "redemption" and "conversion" are in that category. It is a pity that narrow interpretations take words like these over for they are the very meat of mainstream Christianity down the ages. They belong to the language of Christian liturgy, the vocabulary of worship and the data of devotion. In other words, they belong to Christians everywhere.

"Redemption" is a healing word that belongs to us all. It is of the very essence of Christian belief. It is a concept embracing the most basic aspects of Christian experience. It is a gateway to new life because it belongs to the language of hope.

"I know that my Redeemer liveth." The very use of these words brings images of magnificent musical expression, for all that is triumphant is part of that text. Taken over from Job, the statement has been marvellously "Christianised" and given New Testament interpretations quite beyond Job's intention and understanding. That does not matter. For the purposes of scholarship it is important to recognise the differences between Job's intention and the extra themes written into it in the New Testament. That said, who within Christianity will not rejoice to confess faith through these Old Testament words, the confession of profound Christian belief and commitment? So what, primarily, are the emphases in the word "redemption" that give it its healing capacity?

"It whispers of sin forgiven." It is deeply associated with wrong being put right, evil being transformed, disintegration being replaced by the possibility of integration. God "redeems life from destruction" (Psalm 103). Israel must be redeemed, the prophets cry out regularly. Redemption is, as they proclaim it, an act of God himself. Taken on into the New Testament, the "act of God" is bound up with — indeed *is* — the Incarnation. The meaning of the Incarnation is bound up with the words, quoted already, indeed several times, in this book: "God so loved the world that He gave his only begotten Son that whosoever believeth in him should not perish, but have everlasting life." But it is also the text that speaks of redemption. In the birth, life, death and resurrection of Christ, the great act of God in redemption unfolds in history. So great healing associations cluster around the word. It is from God's redemptive act that forgiveness comes. "The forgiveness of sins is indissolubly linked with the death of Christ" writes William Barclay. "He gave his life a ransom for many."

"It speaks of new opportunity", the .opportunity of relationship with God restored. The whole of Paul's understanding of the Gospel is related to the restoration of the right relationship with God, damaged by man's sin. This is God's will for mankind. In the marvellous "myths" of Genesis, there is the record of humanity's mistake. Man and woman together fell victim to the tempting assurance: "You should be as God." The abuse of freedom by the children of God upset the balance of relationship willed by God — of Creator with the created, of Father with children — and only Divine grace can restore that relationship. It is that "act of God" in Jesus Christ, in other words, redemption, that opens the door to healing and to reconciliation. Redemption *is* a healing word.

"It sings of freedom" — the freedom implicit in the newly changed life. Redemption, like the forgiveness which is part of it, deals with the past, the now and the future, and makes it possible to grow in grace and "in the likeness of Jesus

Christ." It opens interior doors, releases creativity and offers true liberty. It must therefore "shout hope." So with this great word "redemption", we have not only the great opportunities of this life in terms of justification and sanctification — that is of peace with God and growth in God, but we have a foretaste of the glory that is to be.

I want to look now at the concept of "redemption" using more the language of psychology. To make bridges between theology and psychology is important at a time when there is a tendency to "psychologise" everything and in so doing destroy so much that is essentially spiritual.

The old-time song "Me and my Shadow" leads us into the language of psychology for it takes us into the Jungian description of the negative side of our unconscious life as the "shadow" side, to which I have referred several times. I have mentioned this word, in this sense, already but would now like to move a little closer to it.

Redemption, that is the process of "justification", of "conversion", of "accepting Christ", along with "sanctification" as the whole process of "growing in grace", is effected by the Holy Spirit at work in our lives. As the Spirit probes and then penetrates our whole being, conscious and unconscious, we are growing into the maturity that is Christ's. The "resistance" we feel to that permeation of our whole being by the Spirit comes from our shadow side. We accept, in principle, the need for change, at a conscious level (whether we effect it or not) but deep in our unconscious selves the yearning for new life, for redeemed life goes on, prompted by the grace working within us. The "image of God" is built into our very creation so there is a yearning to find again that lost divine image. The longing is however constantly sabotaged by inner forces that bring pressure on us to allow "flesh" to triumph over "spirit", the "other things" to take precedence over the Kingdom of God, and the temporal and material to dominate the eternal and spiritual. So the constant inner struggle between good and evil, between Christ and Satan, goes on. It is in these deep areas of our being that the Spirit must move to heal us and make us whole.

To deal creatively with the shadow within, there are certain steps we must take.

First we must realise that "Me and my Shadow" is a statement about a universal condition. It is part of humanity, as we know it, that (in religious language) "all have sinned and come short of the glory of God." To know that is, in itself, a factor of some comfort for everybody involved in dealing with people knows how easy it is to believe that our problem is ours alone. To find that our problem has been widely experienced often brings some relief.

Secondly, we must do what we can to allow our awareness of our "awfulness" to come to the surface. Many will need help in order to do this . . . through friendship or a therapeutic relationship. To try to face alone "the law in our members" that creates evil where good is willed, and the constant, lifelong struggle against the effects of that law, is more than some can bear. The guilt is overwhelming and the sense of failure can be crucifying. Nevertheless, we must try to face ourselves. Only through this process can we have redeemed all that we despise and reject in ourselves.

Thirdly, we must not minimise our condition. It is fearful to realise how far we can sink, given the appropriately safe circumstances. It is also frightening to realise the evil potential of the "collective shadow" (the shadow side of the collective unconscious). Nazi Germany remains an example in history of this possibility for there a great and proud nation fell victim collectively to negative forces let loose in its midst. The stated aims of Nazism were presented as good ones — they had to be or few would have followed. The awful reality involved made itself known in the concentration camps and ghettoes of eastern Europe.

Fourthly, to deal with evil we must never run away from it but face it. There is no other way. Redemption then involves a facing of the evil within us, in all its force, a standing up to it, an accepting of it. The way to triumph is through squaring up to the evil forces within us and acknowledging their reality. We cannot just deny evil, rationalise it out of existence or explain it away. So Christ could only reach the Garden of the Resurrection by first journeying through hell. "He descended into hell." To meet evil's full force head-on was the way Christ chose to do it. It is the only way so far as dealing constructively with evil is concerned.

So finally the door opens to the miracle of redemption. The worst we are or have is acknowledged and accepted and offered to the redemptive process. So selfish aggressiveness redeemed can become energy dedicated to the blessing of humanity. Lust redeemed can be the source of the love of compassion and the compassion of love. Anxiety understood, faced and redeemed, can become a quality of peacefulness and calm that "passeth understanding" and passes on its tranquillity to others.

The final statement is one psychology as such does not know, offer or necessarily accept, for it is a *religious* statement. Redemption is ultimately an activity of God in Christ through the Spirit. Only in that context is it a healing process. Integration comes only through the Spirit.

Chapter 23

Reconciliation

Reconciliation is a healing word that always refers to the restoration of broken relationship. It must therefore surely be the word the Church offers to the world today. Across the divisions that split the world and violate the one-ness of humanity, the call is clear: "Be reconciled one to another." This is the will of God for humanity. It is the burden of our faith to proclaim the healing, within history, of our relationship to God, damaged by the arrogance and pride of man. God reconciles many to himself through Jesus Christ. This is the Christian Gospel. This is the Good News.

All through these reflections I have emphasised the divine initiative in healing the break in relationship brought about by human sin. It is not surprising then that, when Paul speaks of reconciliation between God and man, he never speaks of human beings reconciling man to God. In II Corinthians 5:18–20, for example, Paul speaks three times of "God reconciling man to himself." In other words, as William Barclay reminds us: "It was man, not God, who needed to be reconciled. Nothing had deserved the love of God: nothing turned that love to hate: nothing had ever banished that yearning from the heart of God. Man might sin but God still loved. It was not God who needed to be pacified, but man who needed to be moved to surrender and to penitence and to love ... It was man's sin that was turned to penitence, man's rebellion which was turned to surrender, man's enmity which was turned to love, by the sacrificial love of Jesus Christ on the Cross. It cost that Cross to make that change in the hearts of men."

This exposition of the healing word "reconciliation" may not appeal to all who read it. Those who dismiss as "God-talk" concepts such as those mentioned above that seem not to be earthed in reality but are only theological words, will not feel at home with the vocabulary I am using. Let me then try to put the point in less traditional language and more contemporary concepts. Suppose we take those experiences of "lostness", "alienation" and "meaninglessness" which are so much part of present-day experience and contemporary writing. Feelings of this kind dominate the lives of many who find their way to psychiatric departments, private psychotherapeutic agencies and counselling centres. Alienation is the experience of being a stranger in a foreign land out of touch with roots, out of relationship with people. There is no meaning in life, no purpose in living, nothing to which to relate that is of more than passing significance.

But is not that the parable of the Prodigal Son in modern terms? It is about lostness, alienation, meaninglessness: about the son who was lost and is found; about being an alien in a far country; about meaninglessness — eating with swine when at home the board would be spread. It is a parable of reconciliation — the waiting Father, not there to rebuke but to receive, ready to welcome. "It was not God who needed to be pacified" William Barclay said in the passage quoted "but man ... moved ... to love ..." This is the way God functions, Jesus is telling us, so relationship restored, reconciliation is effected. There follows significantly a ministry of reconciliation to the elder brother too.

One organisation has taken to itself the name "Fellowship of Reconciliation" and to that name it has a long-standing right. But it is a name too that describes all the Church is or ought to be. Loving God and loving our neighbour is essentially an undertaking in reconciliation. No Christian can "take words" with him in ministry and exclude the healing word, reconciliation.

The reconciliation between God and humanity is possible through what the New Testament calls "salvation." "Salvation" is essentially a synonym for wholeness, for it means both "being saved" in a deeply spiritual sense and being "made well" in a bodily sense. To be "saved" means finding "life abundant", life in its fullness here and now, life that takes in the spiritual dimension and sees wholeness as a quality drawn from sources outside as well as within life as we know it.

Salvation is the gift of God in Christ. It is received in faith. As in the Sacrament, and as indeed in the ministry of healing by laying on of hands, the presence of faith in the sense of response to and willing acceptance of the gift "full and free", is essential to the efficacy of the process. So there is in salvation that divine initiative in Incarnation, Resurrection and Redemption of which we have spoken. Human receptiveness and humble acceptance completes the salvation process. The human "yes" completes the response to the divine "yes."

It is enormously hard for modern men and women to accept the full New Testament implications of the healing word "salvation." "His sheer technological Titanism makes it difficult for man to accept his frailty, his finitude and his creatureliness. There is a feeling abroad that, given time, man will master everything." So Dr. Atkinson comments in his contribution "Salvation" in the *Dictionary of Christian Theology* referred to above, on the essential self-confidence and even arrogance of humanity today. Alongside this technological power that encourages man to "draw on his own understanding", there are present today many exponents of humanistic psychology who discourage the sort of attitude that the New Testament doctrine of man and his salvation encourages. But that New Testament insistence on "salvation by faith alone" is dominant in the Christian approach. "Salvation involves grace" writes William Barclay. "It is" (as Paul writes to the Ephesians) "by grace you are saved, through faith." So deeply within the word "salvation" is the concept of a gift, received and appropriated, a gift that we have neither earned nor deserved.

The healing word "salvation" is expressed in the healing acts of Calvary and the Garden of the Resurrection. Jesus was called "Jesus," we are told in Matthew's Gospel, because he was to "save his people from their sins." The Incarnation is meaningless apart from the concept of salvation for (once again) "God so loved the world that he gave his only begotten Son that whosoever believeth in him shall have everlasting life." The need to accept and endure Calvary is pointless apart from its purpose as an act of redemption and reconciliation. The Resurrection is the confirmation that those acts of salvation within history have brought healing to pass, that "death has no more dominion" over us, that, in the cosmic conflict between Christ and Satan, the ultimate victory of Christ's Kingdom is assured.

But are all these statements mere holy verbiage, "God-talk?" Do they mean anything in the hard realities of life as we must live it?

Let us go back to the modern words already used in these reflections. If meaninglessness be one of the modern maladies from which we must be rescued, "salvation" includes the discovery of a purpose for life. This, the Christian believes, is on offer in the Good News of the Gospel. If alienation is an affliction characteristic of present-day people, "salvation" includes the opportunity to find identity. That surely is a possibility — as people like Paul would claim was in fact the miracle experienced — in the new life in Christ Jesus. If lostness is a symptom of the dis-ease of this generation, then a new "centre" must be found round which the life energies may revolve creatively. The Christian faith provides the focus for living which the faith-less need. So the newer generations seek a spirituality much more earnestly than some in older generations do for the evolution of the latter took place in scientifically and technologically conditioned cultures where materialism was· rampant and political choice was to be determined in terms of the offers of prosperity made by each party. So the search through meditation, yoga and other aspects of eastern religions gather ever greater momentum. The new generations are not prepared to tolerate without question values that glorify affluence nor will they be patient with the humbug and hypocrisy of much that is offered as traditional morality. Salvation, healing and wholeness involve a quality of life more demanding and more radical and with a greater renunciation of possessions than ordinary society is prepared to tolerate. Salvation today is concerned with integrity and integration, with an alternative way of life that is materially unattractive but spiritually exciting. Salvation is not in possessions but is to be found through self-denial and simplicity and greater attention to the cries arising from the deepest desires of the soul.

There is more interest now in "salvation" than there has been for a long time. For this we must be grateful. The worshippers of unknown gods may well turn again to the Christian Gospel with Christ once again being "declared" to them. But let no one criticise the demand for "salvation" as unworthy and escapist. Salvation brings integrity of spirit. It brings integration of body, soul, mind and spirit, but it also creates compassion. The nearer we come to the God who *is* love and the deeper we delve into the creative silence within, the more we shall feel compelled to love our neighbour, comfort the guilty, sustain the sad and calm the tense. So the saved of today will not be found singing the songs of Zion, separated off from society. Just because they have found salvation, purpose, identity and integration, they will be at work in the streets of the city, the tents of the refugees and the transit camps of the displaced, defeated and destroyed. To be "saved"means not only to have found the way to God open and our reconciliation with him, in a right relationship, complete. It means, if salvation is truly real, our being moved to compassion for all the suffering of the world and our undertaking a ministry of reconciliation between man and man, woman and woman, man and woman, age and youth, mankind and nature, and all the severed relationships symbolised so starkly in the Genesis story of all that went wrong in the life of humanity.

Chapter 24

The Paraclete

Come, Thou holy Paraclete
And from Thy celestial seat
Send Thy light and brilliancy

These are lines which come from comparatively early
Christian adoration, a translation of a thirteenth century
poem by John Mason Neale. I quote them because they refer
to "The Paraclete" which is a healing word in that it
describes, in the Bible, the Holy Spirit. Through the Spirit
alone, we become whole for, in the end, it is always the truth
that "Integration comes through the Holy Spirit."

Translators have struggled somewhat in their efforts to
translate "paraclete" for the words and phrases chosen have
been varied indeed. We have, for example, "comforter,"
"helper," "advocate," "counsellor," "consoler" and
"befriender" ("one who is to befriend you" which is Ronald
Knox's phrase).

By derivation the word paraclete — *parakletos* in Greek
— means "one who is called" but though that phrase is
passive, the meaning is active. "He came sweet influence to
impart . . ." runs the old hymn. The Holy Spirit is the divine
activity through which we grow in grace. We cannot
ourselves create that grace — as we have noted several times.
The Holy Spirit is "called in" to do for us what we cannot do
for ourselves — and to enable us to attain the wholeness for
which we yearn.

The Paraclete is healing in three ways. First the Spirit is
Comforter in the fundamental meaning of that word. The
Spirit gives strength. The Spirit is called in to strengthen the
faith of the believer, to encourage the process of growth
towards maturity and to support the disciple when weakness

is present. "My grace is sufficient . . ." The Comforter brings power.

Secondly, the Spirit is *Consoler.* We reach breaking points in life — brought on by tragedy, loss, hurt, rejection, pain. William Barclay has a glorious translation of Paul's advice (in Romans 12:12) to be "patient in tribulation." He renders it: "You must meet trouble with the power to pass the breaking-point and not to break." The Spirit is the Consoler when that point is reached for we reach those breaking-points in life and, but for the divine consolation, we would not survive them. "Come unto me, all ye that labour and are heavy-laden and I will give you rest." "O rest in the Lord." "Our hearts are restless till they rest in thee." "The fellowship of the Holy Spirit" speaks of deep consolation to the soul in need.

Thirdly, it is worth remembering the rendering of *parakletos* that stresses *advocacy.* That strand of meaning runs deeply through the word as it is used in the Bible. It is an important strand for it reflects the yearning of the troubled soul for the Spirit to speak, in understanding and sympathy, on his or her behalf. "The Spirit maketh intercession for us." That is good news indeed, for that prayer on our behalf must contribute to our inner healing.

All this is encouragement indeed. To know of new strength at hand, to feel the presence of consolation, to sense that we are not alone but have one supporter and defender — all this must enable us to cope with life at a new level and with a new enthusiasm. Paraclete is a healing word because it speaks of the way we can "triumph still."

Acceptance

The word "acceptance" is a contemporary one rather than a traditional one. It occurs only once in the Bible but the way we use it today is different from that reference. For "being accepted" today carries a particular emphasis that makes it a healing word. That emphasis is biblical so I feel justified in spending a moment of reflection on it.

There are classic New Testament cases of "acceptance."

The first and most striking one is the story of the prodigal son. The image of the father out on the road, forward-moving, arms open wide as the young man reaches home is "acceptance" incarnate. That son was, both in our modern sense and in the New Testament sense totally *accepted*.

These are elements that are common to all situations of true acceptance. Naturally the degree of emphasis varies but the "feel" of the concept in each case is the same. "That we may be accepted of him" (II Corinthians 5:9). The translators include in this phrase the idea of "pleasing " God (see Dr. Barclay for example), but in a sense it is the opposite of the concept that is so important for being "accepted" contains the sheer wonder of the fact that we are received though we cannot please! The prodigal son had been an arrogant failure. The woman taken in adultery had sinned, for Jesus told her to "sin no more." The woman in Simon's house had a bad reputation and was widely known (so it seems) for it. These are not people likely to expect approval from "religion". They had not "pleased" by what they had done. The whole point of true acceptance is that we are accepted when we really feel that we deserve not to be accepted. Acceptance in fact involves, if not contradiction, true paradox. Acceptance is the gracious and grace-full reception of someone, "warts and all."

As soon as we say this, we are back at the heart of the Gospel. The Word that heals is love. We are talking of grace "abounding." We are thinking of free gift, undeserved, and the process is healing. It involves the element of divine surprise. It goes against the pattern of human behaviour where we "get our deserts," for in the realm of grace, just the opposite is true. We do not get what we deserve at the hands of a holy and righteous God. We are given forgiving, accepting Love.

This is the story. This is the song. The Gospel is not about justice — in this realm at least, nor is it about deserts. It is about mercy, love, forgiveness, pardon, grace — through acceptance. The first step in the headlong process may well be that surprise that comes from unanticipated acceptance and unexpected forgiveness.

Such an attitude on God's part leaves us, of course, no alternative. We must be accepting too. If the receipt of mercy implies the giving of grace — as it does: if being forgiven compels us to forgive — as it does: if finding ourselves the happy victims of the divine love compels us to love — and it does — the same is true of acceptance. Accepted by God, just as we are, we must be able to accept others. There is no way out. We have to show our ability to accept others or deny our own experience of being accepted.

It is in this way that the style and quality of the Christian life is determined. It must be, in every area, a reflection of the divine life. It is an expression at a human level of the attitudes and attributes of God. No matter how far we fail to reflect that divine pattern, the relationship between "the life of God" and our living remains. Our way of life must be the way of him who *is* life.

That is the ideal and we know it is unattainable by us. We shall never reach success in this life — if success be the reaching of our ideals. But we need not be discouraged. The Gospel of grace enables us to be "saints," not in the popular sense of holy unworldliness, but in the great Reformation sense — that we are counted as "saints," that is as holy people, only in virtue of the righteousness accorded to us, or imputed to us by grace through faith in Jesus Christ. We are accepted and made into that which by ourselves we cannot and could never be, by the act of God.

It is that position in which we stand through grace that compels us to offer acceptance to others. For the grace-full action of God towards us can only be expressed in one way — a grace-full life of our own and a grace-full love in relation to others.

Because in Christ, we are accepted, we must accept others. In both cases that acceptance implies a reception that is really not deserved. It is, in that experience, that we begin the process of healing. Acceptance is indeed a healing word.

Chapter 25

The Benediction

"The Grace of the Lord Jesus Christ, the Love of God our Father and the Fellowship of the Holy Spirit, the Comforter, be with you all."

"Bene-diction" is the "say-you-well" that comes from God, through his ordained servants, to his people. Benediction is a healing word and ought to be a healing process.

The words of blessing, the raising of the hand or hands in blessing and receptiveness to the blessing ought to make the last act (and it should be the last act) of worship a healing experience. I therefore see that last act in any service as one of the most profoundly moving of all ... and I use the word "moving" deliberately, because there ought to be a real feeling of "well-ness" conveyed in the Benediction, a sense of grace, active and regenerating, a sense of the Spirit, present and in promise. Benediction is indeed a word of healing.

Changed into the word "blessing", the healing effect continues, for blessing is the "make-you-well" of Christian promise.

The idea of blessing goes far back into the Old Testament. The tragic story of Esau and Jacob is focused on the desire for "a blessing." The birth of Isaac to Sarah at an advanced age is seen as God's blessing and Abraham himself is blessed by God, having been "chosen", "elected to service." So "blessing" which seems in its early stages to be associated with fertility and prosperity, has become a process of a healing kind, henceforth to be expressed in liturgical blessing in which the presence and participation of God is paramount.

"The Lord bless thee and keep thee. The Lord make his face to shine upon thee and be gracious unto thee. The Lord lift up his countenance upon thee and give thee peace." So the Aaronic blessing encapsulates the involvement of God with his people in relationship (or covenant) and the desire of God for their welfare, wholeness and true healing. "The priests spread out their hands to indicate that God stands behind them." So later the rabbis expressed this healing theme.

But it is as we pass into the New Testament and in particular to the high point of Christ's life that we move from "blessing" to "eucharist." All the concepts of "being blessed" coming up from the Old Testament's covenantal emphasis are there, but they are raised to new heights in the blessings offered through the life of the Risen Lord, through grace, in faith, to "all who believe." Here the possibility of the healed life, in all its totality, becomes real. Here the supreme "new covenant" relationship is offered. Here is the doorway to the total "prosperity" that we seek . . . the prosperity of the soul. "The risen Lord is the host at each Eucharist and the blessing is his word of power."

Added to this, in Christian thinking, is the blessing that is to be. The final blessing is in the future . . . as we look at it from the perspective of time. Yet in the Christian perspective, time is less important than the reality that is now. We may only "see through a glass darkly," not "face to face." We know only in part, not in whole. But the foretaste is a taste of the reality to come. We live now with experience of what is to be. It will be more glorious than we can presently conceive, of course, and it is inexpressible in the vocabulary available to us in the here and now. But we are "touching and handling things unseen." There is "sweet foretaste of the festal joy." The experience only makes more real for us the sins, the failings, the spiritual disasters of our earthly life, but still "the sons of ignorance and night may dwell in the eternal Light . . . through the Eternal Love." This is Good News. This is the Healing Word.

So the healing words of benediction, blessing and eucharist inevitably lead us to the "keep-you-well" agency in Christian belief . . . the "Holy Spirit's energies." This is the added blessing that forever witnesses to our hope of healing and wholeness for integration is and must be through that Spirit. The "blessedness" of the Christian is to be the more "in Christ." That sanctifying process is the work of the Spirit. "Thou the anointing Spirit art" indeed.

An Appendix

In these pages, and in my *Creative Silence,* I have referred a good deal to terms like "conscious", "the unconscious" and "the collective unconscious." These come from modern psychology and particularly from Carl Jung. They help us to understand something of the way in which personality works — and how processes and pressures within us affect us. For that reason I see evangelism, preaching and ministry as having to take account of and deal with people who require grace in "the deep places" and the hidden parts. I have often referred too to Paul's great statement in Romans 7 because he states as his experience, "The law in my members." This relates as I see it to what modern psychology has discussed so extensively.

In an article in *British Weekly* (December 12, 1980), I described a meeting with the late Canon Andrew Glazewski (whose name I remember only by associating it with its somewhat alcoholic sounding counterpart!) at which he offered me the following symbolic representation of the way in which the Holy Spirit deals with the whole personality. It may help some to repeat here what I said then, but also to add what was not, for space reasons possible then, illustration of that symbol.

Andrew took a triangular piece of paper, set it on the base and described it as a symbol of us all. The top "layer" as it were, he designated the *conscious* part of us. It is the very limited top triangle within the great triangle. The second layer down he designated the personal unconscious. As we go downwards, that is deeper into ourselves, we are in the area of which we must seek to be as aware as we can if we are to be involved in analytic, psychotherapeutic or even counselling work (if it be on psychotherapeutic models), for it is by feelings and experiences repressed in the unconscious that so much of our behaviour and attitudes is determined. The area is "larger" by far than our consciousness can be. It is, because it is lower, also wider and deeper.

The third layer down — again wider and deeper still — he labelled the *collective unconscious*. That Jungian concept testifies to the influences that affect us unconsciously, influences that come from our background, our culture and even from that which is common to humanity itself. (Biblically, I add in passing, compare this to the wonder of the "myth" of Genesis in this understanding of "original sin" — the weight of negative influence that is ours by virtue of our belonging to "fallen humanity — and to the Pauline comments on the "old Adam"). So Andrew Glazewski ended up with that triangular representation of the "weight" of our humanity — the conscious part of us, the unconscious part and the collective unconscious of which we are part. Here indeed are the memories that need to be healed.

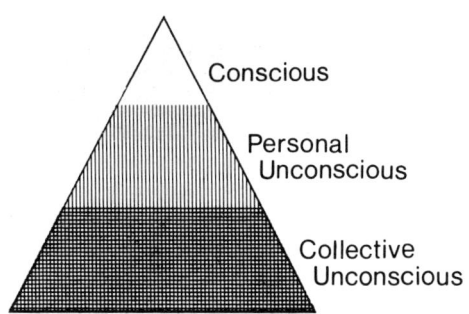

He then took a second similar triangular piece of paper, but turned it upside-down, so that point met point. The upper triangle he saw as a symbol of the Holy Spirit. The meeting of the two points is the place of the encounter between ourselves and the Spirit — where "he" meets "me." But as the triangle moves away from me, it gets ever wider. There is so much more — to the very point of infinity — behind the Spirit I "feel" as it impinges on me. (And it *is* "like a dove"!)

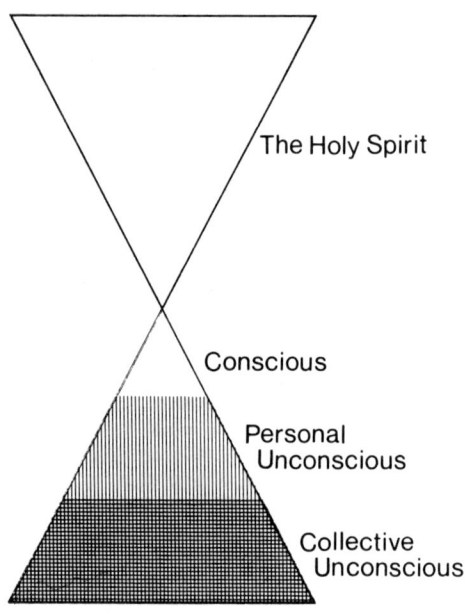

It is the Christian prayer that the Spirit will not only touch me at the conscious level of my being, but that it will move down through all the "layers" that constitute "me." He pushed the top triangle downwards so that it passed through the "unconscious" layer and then deeply into and through the "collective unconscious" layer, bringing the process of sanctification and healing into touch with every part of being. And there, he said, (as you will find if you do this) you have the symbol of the Old Testament, of the Jewish faith, the Star of David. Christ came through that faith because it understood, as no other faith at the time did, the inter-relation of the spiritual and the psychological, the coming of the Spirit to man to dwell in him and to redeem him.

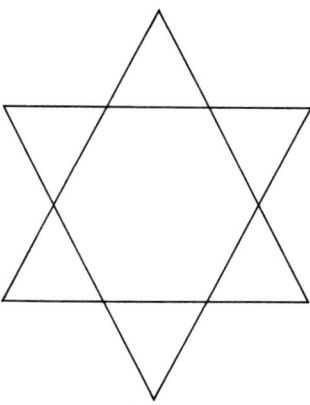

AMULREE PAPERBACKS

A pastoral and devotional series

by DENIS DUNCAN

No. 1 CREATIVE SILENCE, an exploration through Inner Silence to the Harvest of the Spirit £3.95

"It is a lovely book, simple and profound. I hope it is the first of a distinguished series of deep spiritual books for questing seekers after the truth. I shall certainly recommend it to those I meet on the way" — *Martin Israel*

"Should help many to shape a profitable 'quiet time' or longer 'retreat' " — *Charles Duthie*

"Immensely helpful book ..." — *Pennine Radio*

"... of help to all who seek to develop their devotional life ... serves the purpose well" — *Medical Book News, Bombay*

"Remarkably simple and straightforward" — *Radio Hallam*

"Extra-ordinary book ... valuable guided meditations" — *Frank Cumbers*

"A must for true seekers of the way ...." — *Science of Thought Review*

"Although the writer knows his Jung and Freud, there is a refreshing absence of jargon ... I felt better after reading it" — *Graham Dowell*

"It will serve well to lead to quieter hours with God" — *Christian Century, U.S.A.*

"Of genuine value to all who are seeking a deeper and more intense spiritual experience" — *Christian Herald*

No. 2 and No. 3 A DAY AT A TIME, an anthology of thoughts and prayers for each day of a year (in two parts, January to June and July to December) £3.25, *each part*

"A miracle of conciseness" — *Ronald Adkins*

"Deep knowledge of the Bible with facility in writing" — *Church Times*

"Stabilising and stimulating aid to Christian living" — *Charles Duthie*

"The style is simple. The thoughts are deep" — *Presbyterian Herald*

"Warmly commended" — *Manchester Evening News*

"Admirably disciplined" — *Church of England Newspaper*

"A mature book and a very rich one" — *Life and Work*

"Warmly welcomed ... it will bring blessing to many" — *Chrism*

The themes of the months

JANUARY: Love Divine, FEBRUARY: The Loving Way, MARCH: Come, let us worship, APRIL, Sharing and Caring, MAY: Good News-points, JUNE: Deep-down Things, JULY: Firm Foundations, AUGUST: When all is dark ... SEPTEMBER: I triumph still! OCTOBER: The Spirit and the Silence, NOVEMBER: Healing Power, DECEMBER: God with us.

No. 4 LOVE, the Word that heals £3.95

Amulree Paperbacks are published by

ARTHUR JAMES, THE DRIFT, EVESHAM, WORCS., ENGLAND